Mormonism and Masonry

By

S.H. GOODWIN

Origins, Connections and Coincidences Between

Mason and Mormon Temple/Templar Rituals

(1920)

INTRODUCTION

PLACE is made here for a brief discussion of several disconnected, though essential particulars, which cannot well be presented in the chapters that follow.

The first contact of Mormonism with Masonry antedated the Nauvoo period by somewhat more than fifteen years. In fact, the present writer is convinced that the years which saw the preparation and publication of the "Golden Bible" of this new faith, also witnessed the very material prenatal influence of Masonry upon Mormonism, proof of which lies thickly sprinkled over the pages of the Book of Mormon.

This phase of the subject has been treated elsewhere, and at some length, by the writer of these lines, and only so much of the story will be repeated here as may seem to be necessary to provide needed background for certain facts in the present study.

In September, 1826, one William Morgan disappeared from his home in Batavia, New York, and so far as reliable records show, was never thereafter seen by family or friends. But for two circumstances this incident would have attracted no more than passing notice, for William Morgan was not a man in whose movements or fortunes the public was likely to have any particular interest.

But gossip had it that he was at work upon an expose of Masonry and that Miller, the proprietor of the local newspaper, was to print the book and share in the profits of the venture. Rumor was also responsible for the information that certain Freemasons, members of the lodge in that village, had vowed that Morgan's book should never see the light of day. These, in conjunction with subsequent events, closely connected therewith, were the immediate cause of that unparalleled outburst of anti-Masonic excitement (which had been slowly preparing for two decades, or more), that swept the people of western New York far beyond the pale of reason, spread west, and south, and east in its devastating course, and wherever it came, it left no person, or relationship; or institution as it found them.

To one at this distance, that episode in our history appears to have been much more than an ebullition of emotion-it has more the aspect of a deep-seated disease, a peculiar paranoia, in fact, from which none, whatever his rank or attainments, escaped.

At Manchester, not many miles distant from Batavia, Joseph Smith, Sr., had his home. So far as known there was nothing in the character or environment of this family to lead one to suppose that any of its members remained untouched by the tremendous agitation which so visibly affected all others. Indeed, from the characteristics of the several members of this family, as these have been detailed by those who are supposed to have first-hand information, they would appear to be peculiarly susceptible to such influences.

Joseph Smith, Jr., the future prophet, was nearing his twenty-first year at the outbreak of the Morgan furor. He, in common with his neighbors, we must believe, was thoroughly familiar with all the stories afloat, for these tales more and more supplanted every other topic of conversation and filled the columns of. the newspapers of the day. He, with others no doubt, attended the anti-Masonic mass meetings which were of frequent occurrence and of increasing and absorbing interest. He must often have listened to the highly colored and vicious attacks on the Fraternity which marked every public gathering of those days, and many times have witnessed the burlesquing of Masonry and the alleged exemplification of various degrees by renouncing Masons. In fact, there is no reason for thinking that his experietice would be different, in any material particular, from the experience of those in whose midst he lived.

One year, almost to a day, from the disappearance of Morgan, and while the excitement occasioned by that event was still moving toward its peak, the "golden plates" were committed to the keeping of Joseph Smith. The work of "translation," however, did not begin for some months. The book was made ready for the press, and copyrights secured by "Joseph Smith, Jr., Author and Proprietor," in the latter part of June, 1829, and was ready for distribution early in the following year.

A glance at the dates given ---1827-1829--- shows that while the prophet was busy at his task, the fires of anti-Masonic hatred were burning fiercer and fiercer, for they did not reach their maximum until after the Book of Mormon had been given to the world.

To the writer, the evidence of the Mormon prophet's reaction to the anti-Masonic disturbance is as clear and conclusive in the Book of Mormon, as is that which points out, beyond controversy, the region in which that book was produced, and establishes the character of the religious, educational and social conditions which constituted the environment of Joseph Smith.

The reader is asked to bear in mind the facts of the foregoing paragraphs when weighing the claims made of the supernatural origin of the Temple ceremonies. If the writer is not mistaken, those facts suggest a natural and rational explanation of the statement often repeated by church writers, and copied by others, to the effect that when the prophet became a Mason, "he was able to work right ahead of them all."(1)

In any consideration of the general subject, "Mormonism and Masonry," the advocate of the closed door between these organizations will be told, by a few, at least, that in maintaining this position he flies squarely in the face of two of the basic principles of our institution. These are its universality and its non-interference with the religious beliefs or opinions of those who seek to enter its portals.

But, by "universality" we do not mean that every man can be, or should be, a Mason. To take that position is absurd on the face of it. In practice it would mean that every provision relating to qualifications of petitioners must be swept from our codes and by-laws, for they would be meaningless, and that Grand Masters would no longer be harassed for dispensations to permit the application for the degrees of one who is minus the tip of the little finger, or whose left leg is a hair's breadth shorter than the right one.

Often Masonic orators dwell in glowing terms on the fact that our Fraternity is made up of "selected material," of "picked men"---and in a very real sense that is true. But that being true, in any sense, what becomes of this doctrine of universality?

So also with reference to the second ground of criticism, namely, that in drawing the line against the admission of members of the Latter Day Saints' organization we are shattering a time-honored principle of Masonry; we are excluding would-be petitioners on account of their religion. A little reflection, based upon information that has been derived from investigation, will show that such criticism is not well founded. This phase of the subject cannot be argued here: the reader is referred to the succeeding chapters of this book for evidence in support of this statement. But room must be made for certain observations pertinent to the subject.

A matter with reference to which there appears to be not a little of confusion in the minds of Masons, quite generally, pertains to the extent and character of the religious requirements which may properly find place in Masonry. With surprising frequency one hears the statement that Masonry does not con-

cern itself with the beliefs of a petitioner, beyond ascertaining that he accepts the one dogma, of belief in God. Many teachers of things Masonic, including Grand Masters, do not hesitate to affirm that our institution keeps hand off everything touching a man's religious beliefs. But is that true, in practice? This writer ventures to assert that it is not true, and further, he is willing to go on record as holding that if the occasion required it, he could make good his contention by testimony drawn from many of the jurisdictions in which this doctrine is proclaimed, and do this to the satisfaction of any impartial jury.

For a suggestive and interesting illustration of the lengths to which Masonic teachers may go, while proclaiming the sole requirement of avowal of belief in the "one dogma," the interested Craftsman is referred to Mackey's nineteenth, twentieth and twenty-first "Landmarks," and he is advised to make a careful analysis of those three propositions.

A certain delightfully interesting and inspiring teacher of teachers, has a fascinating chapter under the caption: "On a Certain Blindness in Human Beings." Due to some vagrant chain of association, that chapter-heading flashed a signal to the writer as he turned in thought toward the unaccountable attitude of some intelligent people with respect to the matters presented in this volume. Reference here is to those Masons who assume that this subject can have only an academic interest for those who do not live in Utah; in other words, that it is of local concern, only!

Let the fact be borne in mind, in passing, that the Latter Day Saints have missions in practically every state in the union; that students from this state are to be found in many of the eastern colleges and universities, and that no year passes in the course of which members of that organization do not apply for, and receive, degrees in one, or all the branches of Masonry in some of these foreign jurisdictions. Space limitations restrict the writer to the briefest possible suggestions by way of indicating the untenableness of the position referred to.

It is local, true enough, if clandestine, and the application for Masonic degrees by members of a clandestine organization, concern only the Craft of a single jurisdiction.

If the acceptance of a plurality of gods, who are exalted men-including male and female deities-endowed with all the "parts and passions" of men, including procreative powers and functioning in this particular, meets the requirements of all other jurisdictions.

If the Bible on the altar is simply a pleasant memory, or a mere vestigial reminder of what once held place in Anglo-Saxon Masonry, long since superceded by the more recent utterances of the "living oracles," who speak for God, and as God, and whose words are of greater value than "all the bibles put together."

If the Old Regulation, numbered four, no longer has any significance. That specifies, as a necessary

qualification of one who would be 'made a Mason, that he "must be also his own master." How can that requirement be met by one who admits, must admit, that another is authorized, by any power whatsoever, to direct him in all things, spiritual and temporal?

If these and other considerations of similar import are of no concern to Masonry at large, then it may be true that this is a local matter only-but not otherwise.

(1) Seq. p. 42, Note 6.

MORMONISM AND MASONRY

CHAPTER I

Laying foundations; rapid growth; introduction of Masonry; how this step was regarded by Masons elsewhere; forces that unfavorably affected Nauvoo Masonry.

IN the latter part of April, 1839, the first steps were taken toward the establishment in Illinois, of a semi-theocratic community under the leadership of Joseph Smith, the Mormon prophet. Similar attempts had been made by this teacher of a new' faith at Kirkland, Ohio, and at several points in the state of Missouri, all of which had come to a disastrous conclusion. The why of these failures does not lie within the province of these chapters.

On the date named certain of the Mormon leaders came up from Quincy, some fifty miles down the Mississippi River, whither they had fled from their troubles in Missouri,(1) and definitely fixed upon a location for a new settlement. The site of this new Zion included the straggling village of Commerce.

On the first of May, the initial purchase of land was made by a committee headed by Joseph Smith. Soon other extensive holdings were secured and a year later, when a post office was established there, the Postmaster General rechristened the place "Nauvoo," in deference to the wishes of the settlers.

To this chosen spot came the Saints in large numbers, especially from Missouri, where multiplied troubles had beset them. In consequence of this movement Nauvoo experienced a phenomenal growth, for those times. Within two years from the date of the first purchase of land by Joseph Smith the population had grown from almost nothing to more than three thousand, and when Grand Master Jonas instituted Nauvoo Lodge, March 15th, 1842, between eight and ten thousand people made their homes there. Three years later Nauvoo enjoyed the distinction of being the largest city in the state of Illinois, and, with the exception of St. Louis, it had no rival in the Northwest.

These people, for the most part, came originally from the older sections of the country and from foreign lands, more particularly from England, and were largely the fruits of the aggressive missionary policy which has distinguished this church from its inception.

Among those who were attracted by the proclamation of this new evangel were a number who were, or had been, members of the Masonic fraternity. Prominent among these were Dr. John C. Bennett, an Ohio Mason; Heber C. Kimball, one of the first apostles and a trusted friend of both Joseph Smith and Brigham Young, who had received the degrees at Victor, New York; Hyrum Smith, the prophet's older brother, who likewise was a New York Mason, and others. Of this number, too, was W. W. Phelps, a renouncing Mason of the anti-Masonic period and for a time, at least, a bitter foe of the Fraternity.(2)

Early in the summer of 1841 these Masons addressed a communication to Bodley Lodge No. 1, located at Quincy, in which they asked for the usual recommendation in order that they might establish a lodge at Nauvoo. This request was denied, the reason assigned by Bodley Lodge being that "* * * as these persons are unknown to this Lodge as Masons, it was thought prudent not to do so." A recent writer informs us that not only was the recommendation withheld, but also that Bodley Lodge protested against the granting of a dispensation to the Nauvoo brethren.(3) However that may be, on October 15, 1841, ten days after the close of Grand Lodge, Grand Master Jonas issued a dispensation authorizing a lodge at Nauvoo, and five months later, March 15, 1842, he paid an official visit to that place and set the lodge to work.

In this connection it may not be amiss to note the fact that the Grand Lodge of Illinois was barely one year old when the Nauvoo dispensation was granted, and that there were few, if any, over one hundred members in the constituent lodges of the state. The natural desire for increase of numbers may have influenced the action of Grand Master Jonas in this instance. But there were other considerations. The fact should be remembered that he was a practical politician, having been trained in the Kentucky school of politicians during the stormy political period from 1828 to 1833, when he was in the legislature of that state. And at this time he appears to have been a candidate for a seat in the lower branch of the Illinois legislature, to which he was elected a few months after lie had instituted Nauvoo Lodge. These facts should be borne in mind, too, in connection with the highly laudatory letter concerning Nauvoo and its people which he published in his paper immediately after his return home from this official visitation, which covered

three days, and during which he was the personal guest of the Mormon prophet.(4)

From the very first, the movement to establish a Masonic lodge in Nauvoo appears to have been regarded with suspicion and distrust by Masons elsewhere in the state, more particularly by the members of Bodley Lodge No. 1, at Quincy. (5) This attitude may have been due, in part, at least, to the tales and rumors of misdoings which had followed the Mormons from Ohio and Missouri. But there were other factors. The history of the period now under review points unmistakably to certain political, religious, social and personal forces and considerations which were not without a positive and a very great influence on the character and fortunes of the Mormon lodges, and which did much to shape Masonic opinion concerning those lodges and their membership. At the risk of a seeming digression, space must be given here to a consideration of some of these elements of the situation, for otherwise we shall find ourselves without either clew or background.

(1) The following from a "dodger," bearing date of Feb. 28, 1839, indicates the circumstances of these people at the time under review. "Public Meeting

of the Citizens of Quincy." "A public meeting will be held this evening at the Court House for the purpose of devising ways and means for the permanent relief of the distress existing among the strangers who have lately been driven from Missouri, known as the `Latter Day

Saints'; and for affording them immediate aid, as their wants are pressing, a collection will be taken up at the close of the meeting for that purpose." For proceedings of this meeting, see History of the Church, Period 1, Joseph Smith, Roberts, Vol. 3, p. 270.

Missouri contains the center of the Zion of God; there Adam dwelt; there the smoke of his sacrifices rose to God, and to that spot he will return and gather the hosts of God. 75th s-anl. Conf. Rpt., p. 72.

(2) Life of Heber C. Kimball, Whitney, pp. 26-27; Catalogue of Anti-Masonic Books, Gassett, p. 88 ; Hist. of Freemasonry in N. Y., McClenachan, vol. II, p. 518. Records available do not show that Phelps had any part in organizing Nauvoo Lodge.

(3) Reynolds' Hist. of .Freemasonry in Illinois, p. 154; Mormonism and its Connection with Freemasonry, 1842-3-4, Nauvoo, Ill., Smith, *The American Tyler*, Feb. 1, 1905.

(4) The Ashler, Jan., 1860, article reproduced in The Masonic Trowel, vol. 1 of the year following. The letter of Grand Master Jonas was published in the Columbus Advocate, March 22, 1841, and reproduced in Times and Seasons (Nauvoo), issue of April 1st.

(5) Proceedings, Grand Lodge of Illinois, 1842, pp. 52-53.

CHAPTER II

Political activities; appointment of John C. Bennett Master in Chancery; Joseph Smith's pronouncement with reference to candidates; favors Stephen A. Douglas; extraneous influences.

AMONG the sinister forces of the time which reacted unfavorably, politics played no inconspicuous part. With the rapid increase of

population at the Mormon capital came a realization, on the part of the politicians of the state, that the Mormon vote was a factor that must be reckoned with. And the concern of the leaders of the two political parties was in no way lessened when they discovered that for all practical purposes, the leaders of the church could turn the Mormon vote to the one party or the other, as their plans or needs might dictate.

If there lingered any doubt on this score in the minds of those who had reason for solicitude it must have disappeared when the prophet unequivocally declared that he and his people would support the men and party who were friendly to their interests.(1) In consequence of this declaration both Whigs and Democrats sought by obsequiousness and flattery, and by ostentatious acts of service and promises of further assistance, to secure this support. Nor were these religionists slow in taking advantage of this situation and using to the utmost the power thus unexpectedly placed in their hands.

At the general conference of the church held early in October, 1840, the decision was reached to petition the Legislature for the incorporation of Nauvoo. In accordance with this plan a committee, including Joseph Smith and Dr. Bennett, was selected to draft the necessary petition and bill. These documents Bennett carried up to Springfield in December of that year. He appears to have been possessed of some ability as a lobbyist, and this, coupled with the persuasive dimensions of the Mormon vote, operating under the "unit rule," accomplished wonders. When the matter finally came up, it met with no opposition. In the lower branch only one or two dissenting votes were recorded against the measure, and in the senate, none at all. Indeed, a recent writer declares that in the house, the bill was read by title only. Yet, among the members of the Assembly at that time, were such men, of later national prominence, as Lincoln,(2) Trumbull, Bissell, Hardin, Logan and others. And Stephen A. Douglas, then Secretary of State, of Illinois, and leader of the Democratic party, used his influence to expedite-the passage of the bill. . This act, granting charter to Nauvoo, was signed by Governor Carlin, December 16, 1840.

This charter, which "included charters for the Nauvoo Legion and the University of the City of Nauvoo," was of an extraordinary character. The only limitations placed on the powers of the city council were that no law should be passed which was repugnant to the Constitution of the United States, or to that of the state of Illinois. Among other unusual features of this remarkable instrument, was that which authorized the municipal court to issue writs of habeas corpus.(3) This provision, as. the sequel shows, was fraught with danger; it was so liable to abuse. And it was abused. It was the misuse of such writs that brought the city and state authorities into conflict, fed the fires of hatred and opposition, and furnished a pretext for mob action.

About the time that the Nauvoo Masons were taking the initial steps in the organization of the lodge, Judge Stephen A. Douglas, then one of the Justices of the State Supreme Court and located at Quincy, visited Nauvoo, addressed the people, was entertained by Joseph Smith, and while there appointed Dr. Bennett Master in Chancery. As noted above, Douglas had aided in securing the passage of the act of incorporation for Nauvoo, and thereby had won the gratitude of the Saints. His action in the present instance greatly increased his popularity with Joseph Smith and his followers, but it subjected him to severe criticism, and "astonished members of both parties by its indiscretion," the editor of the Warsaw Signal would have us believe. The same writer paid his respects to the appointee with so much of vigor that his strictures drew from Joseph Smith a vitriolic communication, in the course of which the prophet ordered his subscription to the Signal cancelled(4). That Douglas did not fail to appreciate the political possibilities of the situation and to cultivate the. good will of the people of Nauvoo is clearly apparent. On one occasion, for example, he adjourned court,. then in session at Quincy, and went up to Nauvoo to witness a review of the Nauvoo Legion(5).

In connection with the political campaign of that year Joseph Smith issued a political pronouncement, referred to on a previous page, which removed all uncertainty concerning the position of the Mormon people and their leaders with reference to the political issues and parties of the day. In this the prophet declared that the Saints did not care a fig for Whig or Democrat; that they all looked alike, and that he would support those who had shown themselves to be friends of the Mormons. Then he added: "Douglas is a master spirit, and his friends are our friends. We are willing to cast our banners on the air and fight by his side."(6) In the gubernatorial election which resulted in the choice of Thomas Ford for governor, the situation had become so tense that the opposing candidate, Joseph Duncan, felt constrained to make opposition to the political activities of the Mormons one of the chief planks in his platform.(7) The election of Ford was counted as "a great Mormon victory."(8)

Enough has been said in the foregoing paragraphs to indicate somewhat of the methods employed by the politicians of those days, and the sacrifices they were willing to make for personal and party advantage. The effort to win the Saints to the support of one political party or the other continued to be a factor in their affairs as long as they remained in Nauvoo, and it was this rivalry to secure their political adherence that made it possible for them to obtain in return such unusual favors and to wield the influence they did in. political affairs, and it was this rivalry that made them alternately courted and hated by those who would use them.(9)

Another factor which at first blush might seem to be rather remote from the subject, but which none the less militated against the Masonry of Nauvoo, developed in the county to the south of that in which the city of the saints was located.

Some time previous to the date upon which Grand Master Jonas issued his dispensation to the Nauvoo brethren, a campaign was begun to secure the removal of the county-seat from Quincy to Columbus. Quincy was the home of Bodley Lodge, while Grand Master Jonas lived in Columbus. Naturally, the Grand Master was in favor of the proposed change, while quite as naturally the prospect of losing the county seat did not commend itself to the people of Quincy and the membership of the Masonic lodge there. A good deal of bitterness was engendered as a result, and feeling ran so high that when the Grand Master sent communications to the Quincy papers in advocacy of the change, those reflectors of public feeling and opinion refused to print them.(10) Not to be baffled in his purpose to carry on the fight, Grand Master Jonas and some of his friends went to St. Louis, purchased the necessary printing outfit, shipped it to Columbus and began the publication of the COLUMBUS ADVOCATE, the very name of which indicated the purpose for, which it was established. While this furnished the Grand Master with a medium through which he might express his views, it did not tend to mollify the feelings of the people of Quincy. One result was, apparently, that the members of Bodley Lodge lost no opportunity to embarrass the Grand Master, and the lodge minutes and the proceedings of Grand Lodge show how this situation reacted unfavorably on the Nauvoo lodges.(11)

(1) Times and Seasons, vol. III, p. 651. In a communication by Ex-Gov. C. Duncan, of Ill., written in March, 1843, he deals with this very situation in vigorous language. "Let them see," he writes, "the cringing of ambitious office seekers

of both parties at the feet of the Mormon prophet; especially since he published his manifesto, in the shape of a proclamation ....". Miss. Valley Hist'l Ass'n, vol. V, pp. 183-84.

(2) Abraham Lincoln not only voted for this bill, as indicated in the text, but congratulated Bennett upon its passage, and this in spite of the fact that

many * of the Saints erased his name and substituted that of his opponent at the last election. Masonic Voice-Review, (new series) vol. X, p. 261; ' Rise and Fall of Nauvoo, Roberts, p. 81.

(4) The letter referred to reads: "You will please discontinue my paper; its contents are calculated to pollute me. And to patronize that filthy sheet, that tissue of lies, that sink of iniquity, is disgraceful to any moral man. Yours with contempt. Joseph Smith. P. S. Please publish the above in your contemptible paper." Warsaw Signal, June 2, 1841; Masonic Voice-Review (new series) vol. X, p. 262. This letter was dated at Nauvoo, May 26, 1841. A careful reading of the editorial objected to (Warsaw Signal, May 19, 1841) fails to disclose sufficient grounds for so much heat. However, the prophet's communication was given place in the Signal, accompanied by a half jocular, half ironical response, in the course of which the editor dunned Smith for back subscription amounting to three dollars. *Warsaw Signal*, June 2, 1841. The foregoing matters have a further interest in connection with the subject, in that the criticisms of Bennett and Douglas, in the columns of the *Warsaw Signal*, brought a response from the editor of the church paper, in the course of which Bennett is given a clean bill of health. *Times and Seasons*, vol. 11, (June 1, 1841), pp. 431-32.

(5) Historical Record, vol. VII, p. 494, 761. A letter from Joseph Smith, under date of May 6, 1841, which appeared in the Times and Seasons, gives an account of this occasion, and notes the fact that Cyrus Walker was also present, and that he and Judge Douglas addressed the people.

(6) Times and Seasons, vol. III, p. 651; *Sangamo Journal*, June 3, 1842. In the issues of the *Warsaw Signal* for June 2, and 9, 1841, the editor deals with various matters touching the political power wielded by the Saints. Among others is an article on the "Lee County Whig Convention," at which the Mormon delegates, 180 in number, declared that if their candidates were not nominated the Latter Day Saints' vote would be thrown to the other party.

(7) *Historicd Record*, vol. VII, p. 530. Because of Duncan's position, " ... the Church universally voted for Mr. Ford, who was elected Governor:'

(8) *The Sangamo Journal*, Sept, 9, 1842, quoting from the *Wasp*, a Nauvoo periodical edited at the time by a brother of Joseph Smith, a representative-elect of Hancock county.

(9) *History of the Church*, Period 1, Joseph Smith, Roberts, vol. IV, p. xxi., Introduction. *Masonic Voice-Review* (new series) p. 263.

(10) *Masonic Voice-Review*, (new series) vol. X, p. 299.

(11) Reynolds' *History of Freemasonry in Illinois*, p. 174-75 ; Proceedings Grand Lodge, Illinois, 1842, pp. 52-53.

CHAPTER III

Beginning of the practice of polygamy; Brigham Young's statement to Schuyler Colfax; knowledge and practice of the principle extends; de

nials and explanation of the same; Bennett's disaffection.

BUT, while the machinations of self-seeking, sycophantic politicians, and the venom and ill-feelings engendered in an extraneous squabble over the location of a county seat were each influential in the affairs of Nauvoo and its Masonry, neither was as baleful in its effects or as portentous of evil for all concerned as were certain events which even then were taking place within the community itself.

Exactly one month before the visit of Judge Douglas to Nauvoo, when he appointed John C. Bennett Master in Chancery, that is, April 5th, 1841, Joseph Smith took his first plural wife.(1) Although this, so far as available records show, was the first instance of the practice of polygamy, or the "great and glorious principle of plural marriage," the doctrine had been taught by Smith, or strongly hinted at, to certain of his followers fully ten years earlier than this.(2) It was first impressed upon his mind in 1831 and immediately made known to a few of his close, personal friends, who in turn passed it on to others. But, beginning with the prophet's marriage to Louisa Beaman in April, 1841, as noted above, the evidence is conclusive that plural marriage was abundantly practiced in Nauvoo during the two years immediately preceding the date at which the revelation was committed to writing, July 12, 1843. At the time when this revelation was given permanent form, as it appears in Doctrine and Covenants, the prophet had no less than twelve plural wives, and other leaders of the church had followed him quite extensively in this practice. However, it was not officially proclaimed as a doctrine of the church until some years subsequent to the settlement of the Saints in Utah(3).

The fact is worthy of noting here that on one occasion, at least, Brigham Young gave the impression that he was responsible for the revelation on plural marriage. He may not have been careful in the choice of his words, but certainly his language seems to convey that meaning(4).

Although, as stated elsewhere in these pages, Joseph Smith began teaching this principle, actively, within a year after settling at Nauvoo,(5) he proceeded with the utmost caution. At first he confided it only to those in whom he had absolute confidence, and not to them until after he had exacted from them the most solemn assurances that they would keep the secret inviolable, for it was not yet lawful to proclaim it within hearing of the multitude. And secrecy was enjoined for the further reason that not only would this doctrine run counter to the traditions and prejudices of many of the Saints, but its proclamation would place a powerful weapon in the hands of their enemies(6). However, the prophet did venture to test the feelings of the people concerning this doctrine, some time prior to the return of the apostles from Europe, namely, before July 1, 1841. On the occasion named he preached a sermon on the "Restoration of All Things," in which he strongly hinted that the "patriarchal, or plural order of marriage, as practiced by the ancients, would again be established." We learn that this statement created great excitement and consternation among those who heard the discourse, delivered at a morning service, so much so, in fact, that the prophet "deemed it wisdom, in the afternoon, to modify his statements by saying that possibly the Spirit had made the time seem nearer than it really was, when such things would be restored."(7)

But, though the prophet taught this doctrine in secret, and so far as possible guarded against a general knowledge of the same, he did not hesitate to bring pressure to bear to secure converts to its practice among those who were high in church esteem and authority. Three times he ordered his staunch friend and comrade Heber C. Kimball-"to go and take a certain woman as his wife" (plural) and finally, "Heber was told by Joseph that if he did not do this he would lose his apostleship and be dammed."(8)

From the evidence in hand the facts appear to be that, although at this time, that is, during the first half of the year 1841, a knowledge and an acceptance of the doctrine of a plurality of wives were confined to the leaders and principal men in the church, and that not all of them had been enlightened in this respect, within two years information on the subject had been quite generally disseminated among the people.(9)

To believe that such a revolutionary practice could be taught and indulged in for any considerable length of time, and restrict a knowledge of that fact to those for whom it was intended; would place too great a tax upon our credulity, and would flatly contradict the teaching of experience concerning human nature. Besides, the presence of "apostates" in the community, and in adjoining settlements, some of whom had stood high in the councils of the church, would preclude the possibility of maintaining secrecy.. Gradually, knowledge of what was going on in respect to plurality of wives percolated throughout the community, and was taken up and given trumpet-voice by the enemies of the church.

The "enforced secrecy which a reasonable prudence demanded," with reference to the promulgation and practice of the doctrine of plural marriage, bore fruit in another perplexing and troublesome situation for the prophet and his followers, for it gave color to the charge of bad faith and double-dealing. The fact that the leaders of the church, and others prominent in its affairs, were practicing polygamy was a matter of common belief, if not of general knowledge. Yet, those same leaders did not hesitate 'to deny, directly and by implication, that such was the case, and to do this in such terms as to leave no room for any other construction. This conflict between the public utterances and the practices of Joseph Smith and others was used with telling effect by those who, for one reason or other, had entered the lists against the Mormons. A present-day historian and member of the church when considering the particular facts under review, regretfully admits that "wicked men took advantage of the situation and brought sorrow to the hearts of the innocent and reproach upon the church."(10)

An incident that occurred a few months before the prophet's death illustrates the lengths to which the leaders would go in the matter of denials of this doctrine as having any place in the faith or practice of the Latter Day Saints, and may not unfairly be characterized as involving duplicity. It appears that an elder of the church, who had been taught this principle, was sent up into Lapeer County, Michigan, as a missionary. Whatever may have been the character of the instructions he was given, with reference to teaching this principle, his zeal outran his discretion. His preaching of the new evangel created such a stir in that region that the prophet was constrained to take official notice of the situation. This he did by publishing the following "Notice" in the church paper:

"As we have lately been credibly informed, that an elder of the Church of Jesus Christ of Latter-Day Saints by the name of Hiram Brown, has been preaching Polygamy, and other false and corrupt doctrines, in the county of Lapeer, state of Michigan.

"This is to notify him and the church in general, that he has been cut off from the Church, for his iniquity; and he is further notified to appear at the Special Conference on the 6th of April next, to answer to these charges.

JOSEPH SMITH

HYRUM SMITH

Presidents of Said Church."(11)

When that "Notice" appeared in the *Times and Seasons*, both of the men whose names were attached to it were teaching and practicing polygamy, and Joseph Smith was the husband of not less than twenty wives.(12)

In effect, that would seem to be a fairly plain denial of polygamy, as having any part or place in the church system of precept or practice. Other examples of denials, quite as pointed as the one given, and if anything, even more emphatic, are to be found in the literature of the church, some years after the prophet's death. It appears, however, that such statements, and even the paragraphs in Doctrine and Covenants which deal with monogamy, are not to be considered as denials of the principle by church leaders, but rather, as "an evasion to satisfy popular clamor."(13)

Undoubtedly the disaffection of Dr. John C. Bennett, which occurred early in May, 1842, did more to focus attention upon the practice of polygamy by Joseph Smith and others in Nauvoo than any other event. The estimate one shall place on the character of this man, or how he shall be regarded, in the light of the strangely contradictory testimony concerning him, is not material to the purpose in view. He appears to have been a very devil incarnate, or a gentleman and a scholar, according to the point of view, or

end to be served.(14) This much appears to be beyond dispute: he told the truth, and not "wicked lies about Joseph," when he asserted that the prophet taught doctrines in secret that he dared not make public; that lie practiced polygamy and taught the principle in private and denounced it publicly; that one of his plural wives was Louisa Beaman, and that he assured his followers that "It is your privilege to have all the wives you want."(15) The fact is equally beyond dispute that Bennett was in a position greatly to injure Joseph Smith, and no less certain that he used that power to the utmost. Indeed, the statement has been made by a recent writer that Bennett, more than any other person or influence, was responsible for the downfall of the Mormon power and church in Illinois.(16)

One needs but to be reminded of the important part Bennett had played in church and community life to appreciate the character and extent of the peculiar power he held in his hands, and to understand why the prophet hastened to use such means as were available to discredit him before the world, in advance of the final rupture. For nearly, or quite, a year and a half, Bennett had been in a position to know the inner counsels of the leaders of the church, for he was himself one of those leaders. When he became a member of the church, he was Quarter Master General of the state of Illinois. He helped to draft the famous charters, and the bill for the incorporation of Nauvoo, and himself carried them up to Springfield, and successfully urged the passage of the act. He had served as the first mayor of Nauvoo under the new charter; he was second in command in the Nauvoo Legion; he had been appointed Master in Chancery by Judge Stephen A: Douglas, and for a time, he occupied Sidney Rigdon's place as a member of the first presidency of the church, and with all the rest, he appears to have practiced his profession, that of a physician. By means of these various points of contact he would know-could not help knowing-what was going on in church and community.

That Joseph Smith did not underestimate Bennett's power to do harm is apparent in the unusual steps taken to counteract his influence. Through lodge, church, legion, and city council-in all of which he had played a prominent part-the prophet moved to humiliate, discredit and overwhelm him. Finding these means insufficient to accomplish the ends sought, he called a special conference of the church, which assembled in Nauvoo early in August, of that year, "for the purpose of calling a number of elders to go out in different directions and by their preaching deluge the states with a flood of truth, to allay the excitement which had been raised by the falsehoods put in circulation by John C. Bennett." Nearly four hundred men volunteered to do this work.(17)

On his part, Bennett left no stone unturned that promised to be of service in his struggle with the prophet. He used voice and pen so persistently and effectively that Joseph Smith decided it to be the part of wisdom to go into seclusion for a time, to avoid officers from Missouri, whose attention had again been turned toward Nauvoo, by Bennett's representations. For almost a month, immediately preceding the special conference referred to above, no one, outside of his family and a few of his closest friends, had any information as to his whereabouts. A passage in his journal gives an animated account of the effect of his unexpected appearance at that conference.(18)

(3) **Deseret News, Extra, Sept. 14, 1852; Historical Record, Vol. VI, p. 227.**

(4) **The incident referred to occurred on the occasion of Schuyler Colfax's conversation with Brigham, June 17, 1865. The matter of polygamy was brought up by Brigham, himself, and in the**

course of his remarks he is reported to have declared that "... the revelations of the Doctrine and Covenants declared for monogamy, but that polygamy was a later revelation commanded by God to him and a few others, and permitted and advised to the rest of the church." From Schuyler Colfax's Journal, quoted in *The Western Galaxy*, Vol. I, p. 247.

(1) Historical Record, vol. VI, pp. 232-33.

(2) Rise and Fall of Nauvoo, Roberts, pp. 114-118; Historical Record, vol. VI, p. 219; Deseret News, May 20, 1886; Cf. History of the Church, Period 1, Joseph Smith, Roberts, vol. V, Introduction, pp. 29-46.,

(5) Historical Record, vol. VI, p. 221; Life of Heber C. Kimball, Whitney, pp. 331-332; History of the Church, Period 1, Joseph Smith, Roberts, vol. V, Introduction, p. 34.

(6) Life of Heber C. Kimball, Whitney, pp. 333-335; One Hundred Years of Mormonism, Evans, p. 474; Succession in the Presidency of the Church, Roberts, p. 120; Biography of Lorenzo Snow, by his sister, E. R. Snow, p. 68.

(7) The words quoted in the text are those of Helen Mar Kimball, a daughter of Apostle H. C. Kimball,

who was married to the prophet in May, 1843. Life of Heber C. Kimball, Whitney, p. 338.

(8) *Life of Heber C. Kimball*, Whitney, p. 335, 336, Note; Compare the prophet's words to John Taylor, quoted by Roberts, *Rise and Fall of Nauvoo*, p. 117.

(9) *Historical Record*, vol. VI, pp. 220-227; *Rise and Fall of Nauvoo*, Roberts, p. 118.

(10) *Rise and Fall of Nauvoo*, Roberts, p. 118.

(11) *Times and Seasons*, vol. V, p. 423; Cf. *Historical Record*, vol. VI, p. 220.

(12) *Historical Record*, vol. VI, pp. 233-34.

(13) *Millennial Star*, vol. 45, p. 435. Concerning such denials, a church historian says that the leaders were obliged to make such denials because " . . . .over-zealous advocates and ill-informed denunciators never truly represented the doctrine of

the revelation on Marriage," and so, "the denial of these misstatements of the doctrine and its practice was not regarded by the leading elders of the church as a denial of the doctrine of the revelation; and while this may be considered a refinement in presentation that the world will not allow, it nevertheless represents a distinction that was real to those who were struggling with a difficult proposition, and accounts for the seeming denials made by John Taylor, public discussion wilt three ministers at Boulogne-sur-Mer, France, 1850." History of the Mormon Church, Roberts, Americana, vol. VI, p. 297. Another high church authority explains: "Until the open enunciation of the doctrine of celestial marriage by the publication of the revelation on the subject in 1852, no elder was authorized to announce it to the world," and so, " . . . . . when assailed by enemies and accused of practicing things which were really not countenanced in the church, they were justified in denying those imputations and at the same time avoiding the avowal of such doctrines as were not yet intended for the world." C. W. Penrose, Deseret News, May 29, 1886, quoted in Proceedings Smoot Investigation, vol. II, p. 967. Another, frankly admitting his own inability to account for such denials in view of the facts, acknowledged that he had "no sufficient explanation of them:" R. W. Young, *Smoot Investigation*, vol. II, p. 965 ; Other instances of such denials are, a letter by Hyrum Smith, *Times and Seasons*, vol. V, p. 474, and Journal of Joseph Smith, *History of the Church*, Period 1, Joseph Smith, Roberts, vol. VI, p. 46_ See also, Joseph F. Smith, *Historical Record*, vol. VI, p. 220.

(14) Historical Record, vol. VII, p. 495 ; History of the Saints, John C. Bennett, pp. 10-35; History of the Church, Period 1, Joseph Smith, Roberts, vol. V, Introduction and pp. 67-83. Less than a year before the rupture mentioned in the text, the editors of the church paper wrote, in answer to an editorial in the Warsaw Signal, "General Bennett's character as a gentleman, an officer, a scholar, and physician stands too high to need defending by us, suffice it to say, that he is 'in the confidence of the executive, holds the office of Quarter Master General of the state, and is well known to a large number of persons of the first respectability throughout the state. He has likewise been favorably known for upwards of eight years by some of the authorities of the church, and has resided three years in the state." Times and Seasons, vol. II, pp. 431-32.

(15) The History of the Saints, Bennett, pp. 256, 287 ; Rise and Fall of 1Vauvoo, Roberts, p. 118 ; *Historical Record*, vol. VI, pp. 221, 233; vol. VII, p. 495. Cf. Wm. Clayton's statement, in which he quotes the prophet's words: "It is your privilege to have all the wives you want." Historical Record, vol. VI, p. 225. With Clayton's sworn statement, read Hyrum Smith's letter to the "Latter Day Saints living on China Creek," in which lie denies that

such doctrine was taught. *Times and Seasons*, vol. V, p. 474.

(16) *Masonic Voice-Review*, (new series) vol. X, p. 334.

(17) Times and Seasons, vol. III, pp. 870-74; History of the Church, Period 1, Joseph Smith, Roberts, vol. V, pp. 71-82; 137-39; Historical Record, vol. VII, p. 500; The History of the Saints, Bennett, Preface.

(18) History of the Church, Period 1, Joseph Smith, Roberts, vol. V, p. 137.

CHAPTER IV

Masonry established act Nauvoo; the Grand Master's report over conditions there; Bodley Lodge No. 1 requests that investigation be made; dispensation suspended.

THE foregoing facts will aid to an understanding of the situation in. the Mormon capital at the time of the planting of Masonry in that community. They also suggest that perhaps the soil in the place was not the best in which to develop the principles of our art. And further, they leave little room for doubt that the irregularities permitted in the lodge room and the "contumacious" treatment of the edicts and messengers of the Grand Master were not the only considerations, although they were quite sufficient in themselves, that had weight in determining the status of Freemasonry among the Latter-day Saints. We may now proceed with the story of the Nauvoo lodges.

As noted above, Grand Master Abraham Jonas instituted Nauvoo Lodge U. D., and set it to work, March 15, 1842. Our knowledge of the circumstances attending this interesting function is, necessarily, meager, but such fragmentary records and vagrant bits of information, touching this occasion, as have survived, furnish illuminating glimpses of some of the conditions under which organized Masonry had its birth in Nauvoo.

Grand Master Jonas., it should be remembered, was a practical politician, and at this time had his eye on a seat in the state legislature, to which he was elected, later in the year. Under the circumstances, he could hardly close his eyes to the opportunity for securing support for his candidacy which this occasion afforded. Upon his return home he wrote a suspiciously glowing account of his impressions of Nauvoo and its people, which was published in his paper, the Columbus Advocate, and a week later reproduced in the church paper at Nauvoo.(1) Among other things the Grand Master wrote: "During my stay of three days, I became well acquainted with their principal men, and more particularly with their prophet, the celebrated `Old Joe Smith.' I found them hospitable, polite, well informed and liberal. With Joseph Smith, the hospitality of whose house I kindly received, I was well pleased."

From the prophet's journal we derive a few bits of information touching the things that are of special interest. Unlike the Grand Master, Joseph Smith was not writing for the purpose of confounding his critics, or of making votes. Under date of Tuesday, March 15, he wrote: "I officiated as Grand Chaplain at the installation of the Nauvoo Lodge of Freemasons, at the Grove near the Temple. Grand Master Jonas, of Columbus, being present, a large number of people assembled on the occasion. The day was exceedingly fine; all things were done in order. In the evening I received the first degree in Freemasonry in Nauvoo Lodge, assembled in my general business once." Under date of March 16th, the entry reads: "I was with the Masonic Lodge and rose to the sublime degree."(2)

From one other source a little indirect light falls upon the events connected with the institution of Nauvoo Lodge.

Not long after this lodge had been set to work, rumors of unusual proceedings therein became current. Report had it that the Nauvoo brethren set at naught certain established and well-known Masonic laws and usages. This gossip persisted and finally crystallized into open and unequivocal charges. On the 16th of July, following, Bodley Lodge No. 1, of Quincy, held a special meeting called for the purpose of considering the matter and taking such action as the facts might seem to warrant. After discussion, the sentiment of the meeting took the form of resolutions. One of these called upon Grand Master Jonas to suspend the dispensation of Nauvoo Lodge until the annual communication of Grand Lodge. Another throws a little light back upon the events connected with the institution of that lodge. This resolution reads: "Resolved, That Bodley Lodge No. 1, of Quincy, request of the Grand Lodge of the state of Illinois, that a committee be appointed at the next annual meeting of said lodge, to make enquiry into the manner the officers of the Nauvoo Lodge, U. D. were installed, and by what authority the Grand Master initiated, passed and raised Messrs. Smith and Sidney Rigdon to the degrees of Entered Apprentice, Fellow Craft and Master Mason, at one and the same time, and that the proceedings of the committee be reported for the benefit of this lodge."(3)

While this resolution shows that the Quincy brethren were not pleased with the action of the Grand Master in conducting a public installation of officers "at the grove near the Temple," in the presence of a vast throng of people, and later making the two Mormon leaders Masons "at sight," undoubtedly, other considerations were not entirely absent. The fact should be remembered that the dispensation granted the Nauvoo brethren was issued in spite of the protest of Bodley Lodge, and after that lodge had refused to give the usual recommendation. Further, as noted elsewhere in these pages, at this very time a contest was being waged between Quincy and Columbus over the location of the county seat, and not unnaturally, members of Bodley Lodge and the Grand Master had taken opposite sides on that question. It is almost too much to ask us to believe that reaction to these conditions finds no reflection in the resolution quoted above.

Whatever the motives responsible for this movement on the part of the Quincy brethren, the resolution brought the desired action. On August 11th, less than six months from date of its institution, the Grand Master suspended the dispensation of Nauvoo Lodge until the annual communication of Grand Lodge.

During the short period covering its activities, this Lodge initiated 286 candidates and raised almost as many. John C. Bennett reports an instance in which sixty-three persons were elected on a single ballot.(4)

(4) *Sangamon Journal*, July 22, 1842..

(3) Reynolds' *History of Freemasonry in Illinois*, pp. 174-75. The matter is worthy of passing notice, that probably it was this action of the Grand Master, in making the two leaders Masons at sight, that led a present day Apostle of the church to write: "Great Masonic honors were conferred upon Joseph Smith and Sidney Rigdon." *Deseret News*, Editorial, July 16, 1906.

(2) History of the Church, Period 1, Joseph Smith, Roberts, vol. IV, pp. 550-552. The prophet could not-or apparently, did not-foresee how this act of his, in becoming a Mason, would rise, Banquo-like, to trouble future generations of his followers. The unsparing condemnation of secret societies, so often to be met with in the Book of Mormon, seems to conflict with the prophet's affiliation with one of those secret societies. This seeming contradiction between teaching and practice in this matter, has frequently sent to church headquarters the question: "Why did Joseph Smith become a Mason?" The present writer, in a paper published elsewhere, has given attention to that question, and in still another study, has jotted down his thoughts on the subject of, "Anti-Masonry in the Book of Mormon."

(1) *Times and Seasons*, vol. III, pp. 749-750; *History of the Church*, Period 1, Joseph Smith, Roberts, vol. IV, 565-566.

CHAPTER V

The matter of Nauvoo Lodge presented to Grand Lodge; committee appointed to investigate conditions; report of committee to the Grand Master; he authorizes the lodge to resume labor; again in disfavor, and dispensation revoked.

AT the annual communication of Grand Lodge, held at Jacksonville, October 3rd, 1842, Grand Master Jonas did not present a formal address, but appears to have given a verbal report, instead. In this connection he announced that he had granted dispensations for the organization of lodges in several communities, Nauvoo among others. He also "made an explanation and presented a number of letters in relation to Nauvoo Lodge U. D., which were referred to the Committee on Returns and Work of Lodges." Those letters, and the Grand Master's "explanation"!

What a priceless boon they would be to the Masonic student who laboriously picks his way back along an overgrown, obscured path to that fascinating bit of Craft history! To this same committee went a communication from Bodley Lodge No 1, on the same subject, and addressed to Grand Lodge. Some of these letters have been preserved-or fragments of them- and reach us, like a half-told tale on a bit of flotsam. We would. have the story completed, with all gaps filled. We would hear the Grand

Master's defense of his action, and cross-examine the witnesses!

After due deliberation the Committee having the matter in hand presented a divided report. The majority regretted that the lodge had disregarded the instructions of the Grand Master-to send up the records of the lodge but expressed the belief that probably the work done conformed to the requirements of Grand Lodge. However, evidence submitted seemed to show that the "intention and ancient landmarks of our institution have been departed from, to an inexcusable extent," but that the actual situation could be ascertained only by an investigation of the proceedings and an inspection of the original records of the lodge. The committee therefore recommended that the dispensation be suspended till the next annual communication of Grand Lodge, and that a committee be appointed to visit Nauvoo, make a thorough examination and report its findings to Grand Lodge at its next annual communication.

The minority report partook somewhat of the character of a "Scotch verdict." The evidence submitted had failed to establish any irregularities, but fearing that such irregularities could be shown, the third member of the committee joined his colleagues in the recommendation made.(1)

A substitute resolution prevailed which provided for the appointment of a special committee whose duty it should be to proceed at once to Nauvoo, make the investigation contemplated by this resolution and report their findings to the Grand Master. He, in turn, was authorized to remove the injunction suspending labor, or to continue it until the next annual communicationof Grand Lodge, according as the facts presented by the committee warranted.

This committee entered at once upon the task assigned to it and in due time reported its findings to the Grand Master. Among other matters mentioned, it found that the "principal charges" made against the Lodge(2), were groundless and without proof to sustain .them. Very grave irregularities, in the judgment of the committee, had marked the proceedings. of the Lodge. One of these was what is now known as "collective balloting," referred to in. a previous paragraph, and which the committee felt, interfered with the expression of individual preference with reference to applicants. Another indicated a tendency, to make a reformatory out of the lodge, and a third undesirable feature was a misuse of the black ball. In review of the whole situation, however, although the committee found much to regret and much to deplore it was of the opinion that the case did not demand that the injunction suspending labor should be made perpetual, but "that justice should be tempered with mercy." It therefore recommended that the Lodge be permitted to resume its work, the dispensation being continued until the next annual communication of Grand Lodge. The committee also recommended that some member of the Craft should be appointed to visit Nauvoo Lodge, remind the brethren of the irregularities to which objection had been made, and admonish them to avoid the same in the future.

In accordance with these recommendations, Grand Master Helm (Nov. 2, 1842, issued an order permitting the Lodge to resume labor, at the same time admonishing the brethren to avoid "the mistakes heretofore committed."

The evidence at hand indicates that the Nauvoo brethren lost no time in taking up Lodge work-after an enforced respite of less than two months-and that most astonishing results rewarded their labors.

The fact should be remembered that the returns of Nauvoo Lodge, presented to Grand Lodge, October 3rd, 1842, showed a membership of 243, and that during the period of its activities, covering less than six months, there had been 285 initiations, of which number 256 had been made Master Masons. Surprising as these figures are, they are a mere trifle in comparison with what was accomplished in the eleven months following the return of their dispensation. Exact figures cannot be given as no statistical report of work done is in existence. But facts quite as significant are at hand. These are found, primarily, in the address of Grand Master Helm who, as is clearly manifest, was very kindly disposed toward the several Mormon lodges.

At the outset the Grand Master very adroitly placed upon Grand Lodge responsibility for return of dispensation to

Nauvoo Lodge-he merely acted in compliance with the implied wish of that Grand Body as found in the resolutions adopted. Then he directed attention to the fact that "the whole matter is again before the Grand Lodge, upon their application for a charter."

In order that the brethren might be fully advised concerning the general situation the Grand Master reported, that this subject had excited a great deal of discussion, both in and out of Grand Lodge; that the action taken at the last annual communication had been severely criticized; that communications had reached him from eminent Masons which called in question the correctness of that action, and vigorously protested against permitting Masonic work to be done in Nauvoo. In view of these facts, and in order that justice may be done the Nauvoo brethren, due respect be paid to the opinions of those who had objected, and regard had for the good opinion and welfare of the fraternity at large, the Grand Master urged that the course finally decided upon "should be marked by the utmost care, caution and deliberation." Then follows this significant recommendation, which leaves little room for doubt as to the feverish haste which must have characterized the operations of Nauvoo Lodge during the eleven months in which it had been at work:

"Should you finally determine to grant a charter to Nauvoo Lodge, and thus perpetuate its existence, I would suggest the propriety, nay,' the necessity of dividing it into at least four, if not more, distinct lodges."(3)

The west facade of the Nauvoo Temple at Nauvoo, Illinois, as drafted by William Weeks, the architect. This Temple was commenced under direction of Joseph Smith and completed by Brigham Young. By 1848, abandoned by the western migration of the Church, it had been reduced to a pile by mob incendiary and a tornado. The Salt Lake Temple, p.44

And that tells only a part of the story. In eleven months the Grand Master issued dispensations for two new lodges in the Mormon capital-daughters of Nauvoo Lodge! Here is the spectacle of a ,single lodge, in eleven months, increasing its membership to such an extent as to make imperative the breaking up of that membership into six additional lodges which, with Nauvoo Lodge, would make seven, and the Grand Master strongly implied that it should be still further divided-eight lodges, say, where eleven months before there was only one! Nauvoo Lodge was certainly an energetic and prolific mother of Lodges! Somehow, figures do not seem to be necessary to give emphasis to this astonishing situation, and the only incident that comes to mind, at all comparable to this, is that one which is wrapped up in the story of the five loaves and two small fishes!

In due time this whole matter was referred to the Committee on Returns and Work. A preliminary report from this committee was to the effect that it had examined the abstract of returns of the three Nauvoo lodges (Nauvoo, Nye and Helm) and found itself unable

to complete the work assigned without further explanation and amendment of the returns. At the evening session of the next day, however, the committee presented an extended report in which it reviewed conditions in all five of the Mormon Lodges there were three in Nauvoo, one in

Keokuk and one at Montrose. One of these, Rising Sun No. 12, at Montrose, had been chartered.

Among its findings the committee reported that the work of Rising Sun Lodge No. 12 was irregular, that its returns were informal and its dues had not been paid. The work of Nauvoo Lodge had been mainly correct, but there were irregularities which the Committee could not understand, in view of what had already taken place; the records of the lodge had not been submitted as required by law; members of doubtful character had been accepted, and instances were altogether too numerous in which candidates had been pushed on through the Second and Third degrees without reference to their proficiency in the preceding degree. Helm Lodge had been guilty of irregular work, and had rushed applicants through without regard to time between the degrees; it had passed and raised candidates within two days of initiation. Nye Lodge had also done irregular work in that it had received petitions for the degrees on one day and initiated petitioners on the next. The Committee found itself in a quandary as to what it should suggest with reference to Nye and Keokuk Lodges. Finally, having considered all available evidence, the Committee recommended: That the charter of Rising Sun Lodge No. 12 be suspended and the officers cited to appear before Grand Lodge to show cause why that instrument should not be revoked.

That it is inexpedient and prejudicial to the interests of Freemasonry longer to continue a Masonic Lodge at

Nauvoo and for the disrespect and contempt shown by Nauvoo and Helm Lodges, in refusing to present their records to Grand Lodge, their dispensations be revoked and charters refused.

That for irregular work and disregard of Grand Lodge instructions and resolutions, the dispensations of Keokuk and Nye Lodges be revoked and charters refused.

The recommendations of the committee; the substance of which is given here, were adopted by Grand Lodge.

(1) Proceedings, Grand Lodge of Illinois, 1842, pp. 52, 58-59.

(2) Just what was the character of these "principal charges" is not indicated by any records available to the writer. The suggestion has been made by another that they grew out of the Bennett affair, and pertained to alleged discrimination on account of religious or political affiliations. See *History of Grand Lodge of Ia., Morcombe*, vol. I, pp. 148-49.

(3) In explanation of this recommendation the Grand Master stated that the number of members was "entirely too large for convenience in working, and is otherwise objectionable; a fact of which they are themselves aware:" The fact appears from the record, . that the Grand Master's recommendation with reference to the additional Lodges in Nauvoo, was in accordance with a request made by

the brethren in that place. Proceedings, Grand Lodge of Illinois, 1843, pp. 85-86.

CHAPTER VI

Grand Lodge orders ignored; Masonic Temple at Nauvoo dedicated; final action by Grand Lodge; closing scenes in the life o/ Joseph Smith; the EXPOSITOR, and its destruction; arrest of the prophet and Hyrum Smith and their death.

THE drastic action provided for by the resolutions with which the last chapter closed, would seem to have been sufficient to solve all the problems connected with Mormon Masonry. But such was far from being the case. Subsequent events clearly demonstrated that it is one thing to adopt resolutions and quite another to enforce their provisions.

The records show among other things, that soon after the close of Grand Lodge, the Grand Master dispatched a messenger to Nauvoo to secure the dispensations and books of the three Lodges there; that both the message and the messenger were treated with contempt; that the request for books and records was denied, and that the representative of the Grand Master was informed that the Lodges intended to proceed as though no action had been taken by Grand Lodge.(1) And this declared purpose, apparently, was carried out by all three of the Nauvoo Lodges, although the evidence at hand touching continued Masonic activities there, is general in character, for the most part.

From the historian of Illinois Freemasonry, we learn that Bodley Lodge No. 1, being disturbed by the situation at Nauvoo finally took steps to make known to the proper authorities the actual conditions in the Mormon capital. The records of Bodley Lodge show that at a meeting held April 1, 1844, the situation was fully discussed, all the available facts presented, and the secretary was directed to notify the Grand Master that the lodges in Nauvoo and Keokuk continued to work, and that notice had appeared in public print that the lodges of Nauvoo would dedicate their Masonic hall in that place on April S, the members of those lodges claiming that they had received no notice of the action of Grand Lodge withdrawing their dispensations.(2)

The journal of Joseph Smith furnishes certain interesting details of the exercises connected with the dedication of the Masonic Hall which are not to be met with elsewhere. Under date of Friday, April 5, (1844), he records that he attended the ceremonies; that about five hundred fifty Masons "from various harts of tote world" were present and took part; that a procession was formed, which was accompanied by the Nauvoo brass band; that the exercises were in charge of Hyrum Smith, Worshipful Master; that the principal address of the occasion was given by Apostle Erastus Snow; that he, Joseph Smith, and Dr. Go forth also addressed the assembly, and that all the visiting Masons were given dinner in the Masonic Hall, at the expense of the Nauvoo Lodge. (3)

An echo of these dedicatory exercises is to be found in action taken by St. Clair Lodge No. 24, Belleville. The records show that this lodge disciplined one of its members for having marched in the procession on the occasion named. The position of the Lodge in this matter was that the brother participated in the work of a clandestine organization, and such appears to have been the view of Grand Lodge, as set forth in resolutions adopted at the annual communication of 1846. The matter had come up, repeatedly, it seems, in the form of questions as to the standing of former members of the Nauvoo lodges, but was not clarified until the adoption of the report of a special committee, to which it had been referred, at the communication of Grand Lodge in the year just noted above.(4)

Another fragment of proof that Nauvoo Lodge, at least, continued its activities after its dispensation had been annulled is furnished by the prophet's journal. As will be seen, presently, certain men who had stood high in church councils, had become estranged, and were dissatisfied with some features of church government and practice, as well as with the arbitrary exercise of "one-man power" by Joseph Smith. They proposed to themselves the task of changing this condition, so far as it related to civic affairs, and to this end provided themselves with a printing outfit, and laid their plans for the publication of an opposition paper. Through its columns they hoped they could reach the people in advocacy of the repeal of the Nauvoo charter, do away with the teaching and practice of polygamy, and bring about correction of oilier abuses complained of.

Such a challenge of the prophet's power could not pass unanswered, and, as it were, in kind. At a council meeting, April 18, 1844, William and Wilson Law and Robert D. Foster were excommunicated from the church, and under date of April 30th, Joseph Smith wrote in his journal: "A complaint was commenced against William and Wilson Law in the Masonic Lodge &c."(5)

Such was the situation with reference to the recalcitrant lodges when Grand Lodge met, October 7, 1844. If there was any uncertainty as to the significance of the action of Grand Lodge at its session the year before, no such criticism would apply to its pronouncement on this occasion. A brief statement of the facts in the case was followed by resolutions which declared that all fellowship with those lodges was withdrawn; that the members thereof were clandestine; that all who hailed there from were suspended from all the privileges of Masonry within the jurisdiction of Illinois, and that the Grand Lodges of other jurisdictions "be requested to deny them the same privileges." Another resolution directed the Grand Secretary to notify all Grand Lodges with which the Grand Lodge of Illinois was in correspondence, of the facts, and to publish the same "in all the Masonic periodicals."(6)

This terminated the official connection of the Grand Lodge of Illinois with the Masonry of Nauvoo.

Records of action taken with reference to. the lodges at Warsaw and Keokuk are to be found in the proceedings for the years 1845 and 1846, but these are of no special interest to us in this connection.

The story of the closing months of the life of the Mormon prophet is one of exceptional interest to the student of the period now under review. And this, not so much as biography, but as a basic part of the story of his people with which it is inextricably interwoven, and to which it gave vivid and fadeless color. We should be drawn too far afield from the purpose of this study if time were given to the details of that story, but pause must be made for such a hasty glance at succeeding events as will serve to round out this part of the narrative.

With the advent of spring (1844), events moved rapidly toward the fatal culmination in Carthage jail. Early in May the prospectus of the expositor made its appearance in Nauvoo, and one month later, Friday, June 7th, the initial and only number of that publication issued from the press. The Expositor was published by the small coterie of men, including Emmons, Wilson and William Law, the Fosters, Higbees and others, most of whom had been prominent in church and civic affairs, and some, even, had been made the subjects, or beneficiaries, of special revelations. Now, however, although insisting upon their loyalty to the Mormon church, they had taken up the cudgels against what they considered the arbitrary rule of Joseph Smith, and in opposition to some of the doctrines he was promulgating, and practicing.(7) The *Expositor* was to be the organ of this dissenting party, and, promoted as it was by men of ability, who had enjoyed exceptional opportunities for securing first-hand information concerning the abuses and evils they proposed to correct, this project was fraught with gravest consequences to the prophet. In the light of these facts may be found a sufficient explanation of tile intense bitterness and unparalleled excitement which this publication aroused, and equally of the prophet's declaration that "he would rather die tomorrow and have the thing smashed, than live and lave it go on."(8)

As noted in a previous paragraph, the first number of the *Expositor* made its appearance Friday, June 7t1. The prospectus issued a month before had stirred up great excitement in Nauvoo, and proceedings of one sort or other had been instituted against the promoter of the enterprise. But the paper itself seemed to sweep the people, and more particularly the authorities, off their feet. The City Council met at ten o'clock on the following morning and remained in session until six-thirty that evening. The entire day appears to have been devoted to the taking of testimony as to the standing and character of the men who had thrown this firebrand into their midst. To one removed by more than three-quarters of a century from the excitement and passions which marked those early June days, the proceedings of the Council are something of an enigma.(9) The men being investigated were not strangers in the community-they were well known there, and, as noted elsewhere, several of them had held positions of trust and influence in church and city. Apparently, they had given ample and satisfactory proof of their loyalty and devotion to the new faille, and lad been acceptable to their superiors up to the time when they expressed dissatisfaction with certain conditions in Nauvoo. Then witnesses were called to show that these men were the vilest of the vile; they were "bogus-makers" (counterfeiters) ; adulterers, highway-robbers, murderers, "covenant breakers with God and their wives," and guilty of nearly every crime in the catalogue. And the testimony seemed to show that these misdeeds were not due to some sudden outbreak of devilishness, but had been characteristic of these men from the beginning of their connection with the church!

No decision was reached on Saturday and the Council adjourned to meet on Monday following, June 10th. Upon coming together at the appointed hour on Monday the discussion was renewed. An entry in the prophet's journal shows that the entire day was given to this all-important subject.(10) From the first, Joseph Smith, who was Mayor, urged the destruction of the printing plant from which had come the obnoxious publication. Nothing appears of record to show why action was delayed until near the close of the second day given to a consideration of the subject. Taking the recorder's report of the proceedings, as it stands, the Council, with a single exception, was of one mind, practically from the beginning of Saturday morning's session. Only ogle voice was raised against the proposed action of the Council, and that, of a non. member of the church. For that reason, perhaps, he was in a better position than the others to appreciate the gravity of such a course, and to shrink from the storm which he could see would certainly follow. He suggested that in place of destroying the *Expositor*, a heavy fine should be imposed, naming three thousand dollars as the amount. The Mayor expressed regret that' there should be "one dissenting voice in declar. ing the *Expositor* a nuisance." An ordinance was framed to meet the expressed wish of the Mayor and adopted by the Council, and this was immediately followed by a resolution which declared the offending paper a nuisance and directed the Mayor "to cause said printing establishment and papers to be removed without delay, in such manner as he shall direct." An order was at once dispatched to the city marshal in which that official was instructed to destroy the press, pi the type, burn any copies of the paper that might be found, and further directing him, in case of resistance on the part of the proprietors, to demolish the building. The orders were executed on the evening of the same day, June 10 ---and the die was cast.(11)

The project of publishing an opposition paper in Nauvoo had come to a sudden end, but not so with the troubles of the prophet and his people. The destruction of the Expositor, under the circumstances, was about the worst thing that could have happened to Joseph Smith and his followers ---it was the match applied to the magazine.

Two days after the destruction of the printing office warrants were secured by the owners of the paper for the arrest of Joseph Smith and the members of the City Council, on a charge of riot. When the Mayor was arrested he immediately applied to the Municipal Court for a writ of habeas corpus which was granted, and he was brought before that court for trial. After examination he was released and the costs of the case were assessed against the proprietors of the Expositor. The same course was pursued when members of the Council were arrested, with this difference, that the Mayor presided over the court, sitting as Chief Justice. In each of these cases the accused were discharged and the costs were taxed against the complaints.(12)

As was to be expected these proceedings in no way allayed the excitement or lessened the force of the opposition which had arisen against the prophet and his adherents. Mass meetings were held in various communities in the county, inflammatory speeches were freely indulged in, and active preparations were made to use force, if necessary, to bring about the arrest of Joseph Smith and his colleagues.

Before the storm which he had so ill-advisedly invoked, the prophet appears to have quailed, and presently began to make preparations to seek safety in flight. During the night of June 22, he and his brother, Hyrum, with two or three others, were rowed across the Mississippi in a leaky skiff, and the next morning O. P. Rockwell was sent back to Nauvoo to secure horses for the two men. In the meantime, pressure was brought to bear upon Joseph Smith to induce him to return to Nauvoo and give himself up, and when Rockwell came with a message from the prophet's wife, Emma, to the same effect, and another messenger placed in his hands a letter from her, he decided to acquiesce. Several of his companions went so far as to accuse him of cowardice for wishing to leave his people in such straits. The party finally returned to the east side of the river on the night of the 23rd.(13) Two days later Joseph and Hyrum were arrested on a charge of treason, for having called out the Nauvoo Legion, were taken to Carthage jail where, on the afternoon of the 27th of June, they were murdered by a mob.

(1) Proceedings Grand Lodge Illinois, 1844, p. 130; 1848, p. 476.

(2) Reynolds' History of Freemasonry in Illinois, p. 244. In the Nauvoo Neighbor, March 13, 1844, is the following "notice," which appears in succeeding issues of the same publication up to, and including that of April 3rd:

"Masonic Notice. The officers and brethren of Nauvoo Lodge would hereby make known to the Masonic world, that they have fixed on Friday, the 5th day of April, for the dedication of their new Masonic Hall, to take place at 1 o'clock P.M. All worthy Brethren of the Fraternity who feel interested in the cause, are requested to participate with us in the ceremonies of dedication. Done by order of the Lodge, Wm. Clayton, Secretary. March 13th, 1844." Between the leaves of the issue of The Neighbor for April 3rd, the writer found a time-stained sheet of paper, about six by seven inches in size, printed on one side, double column, and headed: "Hymns to be sung at the Dedication of the Masonic Temple, on Friday, April 5th." Among the songs listed were, "The God Carriers' Song," "The Entered Apprentices' Song," and a "Glee." Evidently, copies of this "dodger" were distributed to the subscribers of the paper in the manner indicated and to those who

participated in the exercises at the time the hall was dedicated.

(3) *History of the Church*, Period 1, Joseph Smith, Roberts, vol. VI, p. 287.

(4) Reynolds' History of Freemasonry in Illinois, p. 255; Proceedings of Grand Lodge of Illinois, 1846, pp. 328-329. Because of its bearing upon several important matters, particularly upon the Masonic standing of Joseph Smith at the time of his death, the resolution referred to in the text is here given in full. Although this was not adopted by Grand Lodge until some two years after the tragedy in Carthage jail, the principles set forth in this resolution appear to have been recognized and

accepted by Grand Lodge, even before the action taken, which revoked the authority under which the Mormon lodges were working. The resolution follows:

"Resolved, that it is the sense of this Grand Lodge, that suspension of a subordinate lodge by this Grand Lodge, only affects the standing of its individual members so far as they participate in disregarding the edicts of the Grand Lodge after the first information thereof coming to their knowledge, and providing such individuals by their act shall not have been the cause of the action of this Grand Lodge declaring such Lodge suspended or clandestine."

This interpretation of the position of Grand Lodge seems to leave little room for the good standing of any of the members of the Nauvoo lodges who lived or were in Nauvoo during the period between October 3. 1843. and October 9, 1844, when final action was taken by Grand Lodge.

(5) *History of the Church*, Period 1, Joseph Smith, by Roberts.vol. VI, p. 349. *Historical Record*, vol. VII, p. 546.

(6) A curious story is told by Mormon writers and speakers-and repeated by some others, not Masons-in explanation of the action of the Grand Lodge of Illinois in annulling the dispensations

and revoking the charter of Mormon lodges. Feramorz Little appears to have passed it on to Burton, who reproduces it in his "City of the Saints," p. 350. "The angel of the Lord brought to Mr. Joseph Smith the lost key-words of several degrees, which caused him, when he appeared among the brotherhood of Illinois, to `work right ahead' of the highest, and to show them, their ignorance of the greatest truths and benefits of Masonry. The natural result was that their diploma was taken from them by the Grand Lodge!!" To those who do not happen to be followers of the prophet, a more natural explanation of Joseph Smith's ability to "work right ahead" of others, is to be found in the fact that he lived in the very heart of the region affected by the anti-Masonic excitement, 1826-1830; he was familiar with exposes widely distributed at that time; undoubtedly he, with his neighbors, had often seen "renouncing Masons" present at great public gatherings what was alleged to be all of the Masonic degrees; beyond question, he frequently attended mass meetings where the speakers vied with each other in depicting the blackness of the Masonic institution, and rehearsing portions of the work, and also, beyond doubt, he joined others in discussing the one topic of community gossip and interest. During three years of the time in which anti-Masonic excitement swept everything before it,

Joseph Smith was at work upon the Book of Mormon, and his reaction to his environment, in the opinion of the present writer, is conclusively shown in dozens of passages in that book. (Cf. Note 2, p. 422) . The story repeated by Burton, above, had been passed on to Lieut. J. W. Gunnison ten years earlier, and appears in his "History of the Mormons," pp. 59-60.

(7) *Historical Record*, vol. VII, pp. 480, 545.

(8) *History of the Church*, Period 1, Joseph Smith, Roberts., vol. m, p. 442.

(9) See "Synopsis of Proceedings of the City Council against the Nauvoo Expositor, *History of the Church*, Period 1, Joseph Smith, Roberts, vol. VI, pp. 434f.

(10) *History of the Church*, Period 1, Joseph Smith, Roberts, voI. VI, pp. 432, 466.

(11) Following the destruction of the Expositor, "The posse accompanied by some hundreds of the citizens returned with the Marshal to the front of the Mansion, when I gave them a short address, and told them they had done right and that not a hair of their heads should be hurt for it . .. .. . I then blessed them in the name of the Lord." This speech was loudly greeted by the assembly with three-times-three cheers. History of the Church,

Period 1, Joseph Smith, Roberts, vol. VI, pp. 432-433. Compare letters to Governor Ford by Joseph Smith and Dr. Bernhisel, pp. 466-468. From an entry in the prophet's journal it appears that the building was burned at the time the plant was destroyed. lbid p. 471.

A letter written on the following morning by the wife of Heber C. Kimball has this reference to the subject: "Nauvoo was a scene of excitement last night. Some hundreds of the brethren turned out and burned the press of the opposite party. This was done by order of the City Council " Life of Heber C. Kimball, Whitney, p. 350.

(12) *History of the Church*, Period 1, Joseph Smite, Roberts, vol. VI, pp. 4b0-61.

(13) The reader who desires more of detail in connection with the story of the last few weeks of the prophet's life, will find much of material covering that particular period. Only a few references are given here, and .these all give the Mormon point of view. History of the Church, Period 1, p. 545; Historical Record, vol. VII, p. 558; Life of Brigham Young, Anderson, p. 41;_ Life of Joseph Smith, Cannon, p. 471; Succession in the Presidency, Roberts, p. 117. The foregoing references relate to the charge of cowardice. A letter writer, already quoted, whose words were

set down as the prophet with his friends passed the house on his way to give himself up to Governor Ford, gives vivid glimpses of the situation during the last weeks of that fateful June. After apologizing for delay in writing she said: "Since I commenced this letter, varied and exciting indeed have been the scenes in this city I have been thrown into such confusion I know not what to write. Nothing is to be heard of but mobs collecting on every side . . . . . . Between three and four thousand brethren have been under arms here the past week (letter was dated June 24th) . . . . . . The brethren from the country are coming in to aid in the defense of the city . . . . . . Yesterday... was a time of great excitement. Joseph had fled and left word for the brethren to hang on to their arms and defend themselves as best they could. Some were dreadfully tried in their faith to think Joseph should leave them in the hour of danger. Before night yesterday, things put on a different aspect-Joseph returned and gave himself up for trial." *Life of Heber C. Kimball*, Whitney, pp. 350-51.

CHAPTER VII

A study in resemblances; symbols and inscriptions; sources of information; articles used in temple ceremonies.

HAVING thus traced the variegated fortunes of the Nauvoo Lodges, and noted some of the outstanding features of their environment, we are now prepared to enter another phase of the subject which may well be characterized, "A study in Resemblances."

Not infrequently the question is asked. "Does the Mormon church make use of the Masonic ritual in its Temple ceremonies?" For obvious reasons no attempt will be made here to give a categorical answer to this question; nor is it the writer's purpose to point out any "resemblances" that may be discovered. What purports to be facts will be presented-the reader will make his own deductions.

The observant Craftsman cannot be long among the Mormon people without noting the frequent use made of certain emblems and symbols which have come to be associated in the public mind with the Masonic fraternity. Now and again he will catch expressions and phrases in conversation, and meet with terms in literature, which are suggestive, to say the least. If he should continue his residence in Utah, he will sometimes be made aware of the fact, when shaking hands with a Mormon neighbor or friend, that there is a pressure of the hand as though some sort of a "grip" is being given. Visitors and residents of Utah often remark upon the extensive use made of certain emblems, as, for example, the conventional beehive. This familiar figure occupies the center of the great seal of the state; a model of immense size rises from the roof of the beautiful "Hotel Utah," and one of smaller proportions crowns the platform on the cupola of the "Beehive House," once, and for many years, the official residence of the president of the church. It is noticeably prominent on the great bronze doors which guard the entrance to the sacred precincts of the Salt Lake Temple, as well as on doors of commercial and other buildings. It crowns newel posts of cement steps which lead to the entrance of meeting houses and tabernacles, and public buildings, and frequently appears with effect in the decorative schemes of interiors and lobbies of hotels.

Other emblems, with which the public is more or less familiar, are used extensively, more especially in and about the Salt Lake Temple, and, presumably, in all other temples of the Mormon church. On the interior of this building, we learn from an unquestioned authority, there are in the walls several series of stones of emblematical design and significance, representing the earth, moon, sun and stars.

The Mormon "Sunstone" which surmounted the columns at Nauvoo Lodge in Illinois.

On the east central tower is an inscription, the letters deep cut, lined with gold, which reads: "Holiness to the Lord." This inscription, it might be noted, appears over the doorways of some of the business establishments conducted by the church and over the entrance to the church tithing-houses, and it is given place on the stationery used in the official correspondence conducted by church authorities. Immediately beneath this inscription, over the central casement of the east tower of the Temple, is the emblem of the clasped hands. On the corresponding stones, above the upper windows, in each of the central towers, is carved the "All Seeing Eye." Covering the plate glass double doors on the east and west sides of the Temple, each of which is four by twelve feet, are bronze grills of intricate pattern which carry medallions of the beehive, while an escutcheon cut in relief shows the clasped hands circled by a wreath. In the "Garden Room" of the Temple the ceiling is embellished with oil paintings to represent clouds and the sky, in which appear the sun, moon and stars. In the center of this room, and against the south wall, is a platform which is reached by three steps. On the platform is an altar upon which rests the Bible. In the "Terrestrial Room," at the east end, is a raised floor, reached by three steps.(1)

Passing now from this phase of the subject we come next to the language used in a part of the Temple ceremonies. Here we are dependent for authorities, mainly, upon certain exposes, though collateral evidence is not wanting. The exposes referred to here, are three in number, and they appeared practically a generation apart. A brief list of other authorities is given in the notes below.(2)

A careful comparison of the three accounts shows that the first, or oldest one, differs from the other two, or later ones, in one significant particular, at least. The first, or van

Duseri account, presents a larger number of stages than the later ones, and leaves the impression of carrying a larger amount of material that had not been as carefully worked over as has the ceremony more recently in use. This fact seems to point to the conclusion that the work was in a preliminary or experimental stage at Nauvoo, and that later it was developed and perfected into its present form, which included the practical omission of the last four degrees. A well informed member of the Mormon Church, in conversation with the writer, accounted for the character of the Van Dusen statements upon a different supposition-though upon what authority was not disclosed. He said that "Van Dusen was a liar," and further, that "he was a Mason." It may very well have been that, he was a Mason, although no records are known to the writer which support that assertion. The followers of Joseph Smith believe that the Temple ceremonies were revealed to the prophet, complete, and more than a year before he became a Mason, and that proof of this is to be found in the Doctrine and Covenants.(3)

As a preliminary to a consideration of some of the language of the Temple ritual, it may not be amiss to note certain objects and articles used in connection with that ritual.

The garments worn by both men and women during a goodly portion of the ceremonies are of white cloth and of the one-piece pattern. On the right breast is a "square," and on the left, "compasses."(4) There are other marks or openings which are of no special interest to us here.

As used in the Temple at Nauvoo, the slits representing

a pair of compasses, were on the knees, rather than on the left breast. The pattern of this garment, the wearer is informed, was revealed to Joseph Smith direct from heaven, and is the same as that, worn by Adam and Eve. It must not be removed, in which case assurance is given that it will protect from danger, temporal and spiritual.(5)

At one point in the ceremonies, the "devil" comes in wearing a silk hat and having on a Masonic apron. This apron is embellished with two columns, having a serpent suspended midway between them, and another serpent entwined about the base of each. The aprons worn by the men and women are alike, and are described as being a "square half yard of green silk with nine fig leaves worked on them in brown sewing silk." Those in use at Nauvoo were of "white cloth about eighteen inches square with green silk leaves pasted on."

In the old endowment house at Salt Lake, the ceiling of the "Garden of Eden Room" was painted much the same as that described above, with these additions: In each corner there was a Masonic emblem; in one, "compasses," in another a "square," and in the other two a "level" and a "plumb."(6)

(1) *The House of the Lord*, Talmage, pp. 177, 179, 186, 189. See Joseph F. Smith on the "All-Seeing Eye," and "Holiness to the Lord," *68th Annual Conference Report*, p. 11.

(2) Nauvoo and Its Temple, by Increase McGee Van Dusen and his wife Maria. (24 pp.), 1847. On the title page is the following: "The Sublime and Ridiculous Blended: Called, The Endowment; as was acted by upwards of 12,000, in secret in the Nauvoo Temple, said to be revealed by God as a reward for building that splendid edifice, and the express object for which it was built."

The Mormon Endowment House, by Mrs. G. S. R-, Nephi, Utah, September 24, 1879. Published in the Salt Lake Tribune, September 28, 1879, and reprinted in the same paper, February 12, 1906.

The Testimony of Prof. Walter M. Wolfe, given before the Smoot Investigation Committee, at Washington, D. C., and published in the Salt Lake Tribune, February 12, 1906.

A few other references are: Reminiscences of Early Utah, Baskin, pp. 98-99; The Revelation in the Mountain, Major, pp. 120-160; The Tyranny of Mormonism, Mrs. T. B. H. Stenhouse, pp. 192-200; Mormonism, Its Rise, Progress and Present Condition, Green, pp. 41-53.

(3) Section 124. See Note 6, p. (37). The Temple ceremonies were received by the prophet, it is said, from one to five or six years before he became a Mason. Apostle Ballard, Salt Lake Herald, Dec. 29,

1919; B. H. Roberts, Improvement Era, vol. XXIV, pp. 937-939.

(4) The rents in the garments are known as holy priesthood marks, or marks of the temple, and remind the wearer what the penalty will be should he ever violate his covenants or reveal any of the tokens. Proceedings, Smoot Investigation, vol. II, p. 182.

(5) Nauvoo and Its Temple, Van Dusen, p. 8; *The Salt Lake Tribune*, February 12, 1906; Revelation in the Mountain, Major, pp. 121f.

(6) *The Salt Lake Tribune*, Feb. 12, 1906, p. 2; Nauvoo and Its Temple, Van Dusen, p. 11.

CHAPTER VIII

Temple ceremonies; characterized by Mormon writer;
Nauvoo Masonry, as understood by a present-day Apostle;
Temple ordinances the only genuine Masonry.

THE opening part of the Temple ceremonies, which have been characterized by a Mormon writer "# * * as the Masonic sacred drama of the Fall of Man,"(1) need not detain us. Here occur the washings and anointings and assumption of the garment, before referred to, and a representation, in dialogue, of the creation of the world and of man and woman. Following this preparatory part, the first obligation, or oath, is taken. One of the several couples, representing Adam and Eve, kneels at the altar, and all participate in the ceremonies. The audience stands, each with the right hand raised to a square, when the following oath is taken: "We, and each of us, solemnly bind ourselves that we will not reveal any of the secrets of the first token of the Aaronic priesthood, with its accompanying name, sign or penalty. Should I do so, I agree that my, throat may be cut from ear to ear, and my tongue torn out by its roots."

"Grip. The grip is very simple: Hands clasped, pressing the point of the knuckle of the index finger with the thumb."

"Sign. In executing the sign of the penalty, the hand, palm down, is placed across the body, so that the thumb comes directly under and a little behind the ear. The hand is then drawn sharply to the right across the throat, the elbow standing out at a position of ninety degrees from the body;

the hand is dropped from the square to the side." In the earliest form of these ceremonies, as used in Nauvoo in 1846, this obligation, or a part of it at least, appears to have been given in what was termed the sixth degree. (2)

The exercises then proceed. Various characters appear and carry on a dialogue, and then a robe and sandals are put on the candidates, and the apron replaced and the second oath is administered: "tee, and each of us, do solemnly promise and bind ourselves never to reveal any of the secrets of this priesthood, with the accompanying name, grip and penalty. Should we do so, we agree that our breasts may be torn open, our heart and vitals torn out and given to the birds of the air and the beasts of the field."

"Grip. Clasp the right hand and place the thumb into the. hollow of the knuckles, between the first and second fingers.

"Sign. The sign is made by extending the right hand across the left breast, directly over the heart; then drawing it rapidly from left to right, with the elbow at the square; then dropping the hand to the side."

The candidates are then conducted into what is known as the "Celestial Room." Here also characters appear and carry on conversation, relating to the ceremonies, and other preparations are made for the administering of the third oath, which is as follows: "You, and each of you, do covenant and promise that you will never reveal any of the secrets of the priesthood, with any accompanying name, sign and penalty. Should you do so you agree that your body may be cut asunder and all your bowels gush out."

"In this, the left hand is placed palm upright, directly in front of the body, there being a right angle formed at the elbow; the right hand, palm down, is placed under the elbow of the left; then drawn sharply across the bowels, and both hands dropped to the side."(3) The grip is given by "grasping the right hands so that the little fingers are interlocked and the forefinger presses the wrist. This is known as the patriarchal grip, or the true sign of the nail."

The Neophytes are then ready for the three-fold obligation which relates to "The Law of Sacrifice," " The Law of Chastity," and the "Law of Vengeance." The last named law, it might be noted in passing, is given with but slight variation, by all three of the authorities quoted here. The character of the second law is indicated by its title, and is not without significance, though it need not detain us.

Following these obligations the candidates are seated and a long sermon or lecture is given, in which the entire history of the Temple work is rehearsed. They are then instructed in the true order of prayer. In this, when all is in readiness, an elder kneels at the altar, his right arm raised to the square, his left hand extended, as if to receive a blessing. A form of prayer is then offered which, it is said, is used in all priesthood meetings. The candidates are then ready to pass through the veil.

"In the veil are to be seen the square and compasses; also other openings which represent the slits in the knees of every garment." In the room where this veil is placed, there is also a platform upon which the candidates take seats when their names are called, and which is ascended by three steps. With the aid of an attendant the Neophyte gives the required answers and grips, which include the two grips of the Aaronic priesthood and the two grips of the Melchizedek priesthood. Following the last grip, a dialogue ensues...

"Elohim-`What is this'?"

"Neophyte-`The second grip of the Melchizedek priesthood, patriarchal grip, or sure sign of the nail'."

"Elohim-`Has it a name'?"

"Neophyte-'It has'."

"Elohim-`Will you give it to me'?"

"Neophyte-`I cannot, for I have not yet received it; for this purpose I have come to converse with the Lord behind the veil'."

"Elohim-`You shall receive it upon the five points of fellowship through the veil. These are foot to foot, knee to knee, breast to breast, hand to back, and mouth to ear'."(4)

Here we may take leave of the Temple ceremonies, and consider briefly a few significant utterances derived from the written and spoken words of those who, presumably, speak from first-hand information.

First, is language used by a brilliant writer of the Mormon faith. In a chapter that deals with the Temple at Logan, Utah, he contrasts the views of this 'structure held by Latter-day Saints and Gentiles, and then proceeds "To the Mormons the Logan Temple is a grand Masonic fabric, reared unto the name of the God of Israel, where endowments, are given, and ordinances administered, and services performed which concern salvation and exaltation, both of the living and the dead, and connected with the Mormon Church."

After referring to a supposed "Polygamic Theocracy," which he says, is popularly supposed to exist in the Logan Temple, the author continues:

"And what makes this matter of so much importance and interest is that the Logan Temple today is looked upon as the Masonic embodiment of that `Polygamic Theocracy.'"

The author then passes upon the relative merits of two exposes of the endowment house secrets, and continues:

"Meantime the Mormon apostles and elders with a becoming repugnance and Masonic reticence quite understandable to members of every Masonic order have shrunk from a public exhibition of the sacred things of their Temple." When describing certain scenes enacted in the endowment ceremonies, he refers to the Garden of Eden representation as "* * * the Masonic sacred drama of the Fall of Man." And again, "A sign, a grip, and a keyword were communicated and impressed upon us, and the third degree of Mormon endowment, or the first degree of the Aaronic priesthood was conferred."

And finally our author refers to the "oath of chastity," alluded to above, and marks with especial emphasis the fact that "the oath implies that no man dare, under penalty of death, to betray his brother's wife or daughter."(5)

Perhaps the most interesting and significant utterance on the subject, from one who is in a position to know whereof he speaks, is attributed to a member of the present quorum of the Twelve Apostles.. In an address delivered in the Salt Lake Tabernacle, on the last Sunday of 1919, as reported in one of the daily papers, the speaker said "Modern Masonry is a fragmentary presentation of the ancient order established by King Solomon, from whom it is said to have been handed down through the centuries."

"Frequent assertion that some details of the Mormon Temple ordinances resemble Masonic rites, led him to refer to this subject," the speaker declared, and he added, "that he was not sorry there was such a similarity, because of the fact that the ordinances and rites revealed to Joseph Smith constituted a reintroduction upon the earth of the divine plan inaugurated in the Temple of Solomon in ancient days."

"Plans for the ordinances to be observed in the Temple built at Nauvoo * * * were revealed to Joseph Smith, as recorded in the Doctrine and Covenants, more than a year prior to the time the founder of the Mormon Church became a member of the Masonic order. The latter order," the speaker affirmed, "claimed origin with King Solomon, but through lapses and departures, which had naturally come into the order in the course of time, it had fallen somewhat into imperfection of detail. The temple plan revealed to Joseph Smith * * * was the perfect Solomonic plan, under which no man was permitted to obtain the secrets of Masonry unless he also held the holy priesthood."

The speaker then explained that authentic proof in Masonic history goes to show that "the five lodges of the order, established by Joseph Smith and other members of the Mormon Church, had been discountenanced by the great organization through mistaken non. observance of a mere technicality." The Mormon lodges, Apostle Ballard declared, "had been accepting and advancing members in the order by viva voce vote, instead of by secret ballot, as the rule required." "But," he said, "the technical offense had been seized upon as a cause for repudiating the lodges established by members of an unpopular church."(6)

It is not our purpose to examine critically any of the assertions made by this speaker. Enough has been said in the preceding pages, and more evidence could be adduced, to show that the Apostle here ignored some very material facts and that the action of the Grand Lodge of Illinois with reference to the Mormon lodges was due to other causes than the one named by the speaker quoted.

Further, no objections will be urged here to the acceptance on the part of anyone of the statement that the temple ritual, parts of which have been presented in these pages, was revealed to Joseph. Smith, or to anyone else, direct from heaven. The writer will only say that no evidence has come to his knowledge which points to any such supernatural derivation, while on the other hand he is o£ the opinion that in the preceding pages attention has been directed to the real source and origin of the temple ceremonies.

In taking leave of this part of the subject, the fact is worthy of record that Joseph Smith fixes the date of the introduction of the endowments as May 4, 1842, nearly two months after he became a Mason. Under that date he wrote that he instructed certain of his followers "in the principles and order of the priesthood, attending to washing, anointing, endowments and the communication of keys pertaining to the Aaronic priesthood and so on to the highest order of the Melchizedek priesthood setting forth the order pertaining to the Ancient of Days" * * * and that, "in this Council was instigated the ancient order of things for the first time in these last days." This, of course, does not preclude the possibility of the "revelation" of this order having been received much earlier than the date given, as is held by the historian of the church.(7)

(1) Tullidge's Histories of Utah: Northern Utah and Southern Idaho, vol. II, p. 444.

(2) *The Salt Lake Tribune*, Feb. 12, 1906. If this paper is not available, see The Revelation in the Mountain, Major,. pp. 129-160, where the Tribune article is reproduced; Nauvoo and Its Temple, Van Dusen, p. 13.

(3) *The Salt Lake Tribune*, February 12, 1906.

(4) *The Salt Lake Tribune*, Feb. 12, 1906, p. 3; *Tell It All*, Mrs. Stenhouse, pp. 192-200; *The Latter Day Saints*, Kauffman, pp. 155-169; 312-328.

(5) Tullidge's Histories of Utah: Northern Utah and Southern Idaho, vol. lI, pp. 425, 426, 444, 446, 4.50; also his life of Joseph Smith, pp. 391-393. The same author declares: "Mormonism is Masonic," *The Women of Mormondom*, p. 75.

(6) *The Salt Lake Herald*, Dec. 29, 1919. See also, B. H. Roberts, *Improvement Era*, vol. XXIV, pp. 937-939.

(7) Concerning the entry in the prophet's journal, quoted in the text, B. H. Roberts states: "This is the Prophet's account of the introduction of the Endowment ceremonies in this dispensation, and is the foundation of the sacred ritual of the temples." History of the Church, Period 1, Joseph Smith, Roberts, vol. V, p. 2, Note. Roberts follows

this statement: "There has been some controversies as to the time when these ceremonies were introduced into the church." The intelli- gent Craftsman will hardly need to be told that the matter has significance in our present study. :One of the founders and first editors of Times and Seasons, and who was editor-in-chief of that periodical up to the date on which Joseph Smith took the first degree in Masonry, said, "that all these ceremonies were introduced into the Church by the Prophet Joseph Smites at least as early as 1843." Quoted by Roberts, as above, p. 3, Note. Wilford Woodruff, then "virtual head of the Church" (*History of Utah*, Whitney, vol. III, p. 587) in 1887, in a letter which was read at the Semi-Annual Conference of the Church, that year, fixed the time when Joseph Smith gave the endowments to the twelve apostles, as being in the winter of 1843-44. An Epistle of the Council of the Twelve Apostles, Oct. 10, 1887, p. 2.

CHAPTER IX.

Certain teachings of Mormonism appear to be in conflict with fundamental principles of the Fraternity; power of priesthood well-nigh absolute.

UNDER any circumstances great care should be exercised in the selection of material for membership in Masonic Lodges. This holds true everywhere and at all times and is a duty that in an especial sense devolves upon those who in a representative capacity first pass upon the qualifications of applicants for our mysteries in Utah, and the same holds true elsewhere. A number of reasons for this might be given, some of which it is the purpose of- the following chapters to set forth.

At the outset it should be stated that the historic, well known and consistent position held by the Craft of this jurisdiction, practically from the very inception of organized Masonry, back in '65, to the present time furnishes one reason for caution on the part of Utah investigating committees, in particular(1). Further, there is a notable tendency on the part of some who are young in Masonry, and of others who, though older, are inclined to be lenient toward a relaxation of requirements, to take account only of the superficial and to base their conclusions and action upon an imperfect apprehension of facts which cannot be ignored with safety. In what follows attention is directed to certain facts no one of which, perhaps, taken alone may seem to be of any great consequence, but which in the aggregate are worthy of serious consideration. In seeking to attain the object in view we may pass boundaries which, somehow, have acquired a pseudo-sanctity and find ourselves in fields all too rarely entered by those who, for the time being, are charged with the duty of guarding well the outer portals of the Craft.

That there may be no uncertainty as to what is here undertaken, the statement may be made that we are dealing with the general subject of "Mormonism and Masonry," and that the particular phase of the subject upon which we now enter relates to the eligibility of any would-be applicant for the mysteries of Freemasonry, who at the same time is a member of the Latter-Day Saints' organization.

Masonry requires of its initiates, among other things, that they shall come of their own free will and accord. By implication, principle and teaching it assumes that those who come into its fellowship are, and will remain, free, from any influence or power that might interfere with the performance of such duties as may devolve upon them by reason of such membership.(2) In order to ascertain the facts, a petitioner for the degrees in Utah is required to furnish a list of the fraternal and religious organizations with which he is now, or has been affiliated. This .is not done in criticism of any organization that may, or that seems to, curtail the freedom of thought or action of its adherents. Such criticism does not fall within the province of this study, or of Masonry. But Masonry, like all other organizations, both claims and exercises the right to erect such standards as may seem to be necessary; to formulate and apply tests; to pass upon the qualifications of those who knock at its doors, and to decide in any and every case whether the requirements thus laid down have been, or can be, satisfactorily complied with. In the exercise of these and all other powers and prerogatives Masonry is a law unto itself.

With the ground thus cleared we may now proceed to consider certain facts the bearing and significance of which can hardly be mistaken.

Those who are authorized to speak for the church have left little room for doubt that the Latter Day Saints' organization makes such demands upon its adherents that the results do not accord with the genius of Freemasonry.

For example. The utmost emphasis is laid upon the authority and power of the priesthood. A man may not honestly differ from the presiding priesthood without being guilty of apostasy and subject to excommunication. Indeed, this is carried so far that even to criticize the authorities is declared to be a dangerous thing. One should do as the priesthood directs, whether one likes it or not.(3) Such teachings differ not at all, in principle, as the present writer sees the matter, from those enunciated by the authorities back in '69. Said George Q. Cannon on one occasion, Brigham Young being present, "It is apostasy to differ honestly with the measures of the president. A man may be honest even in hell." And President Wells said, on the same occasion, and wills nothing wanting in the way of emphasis: "One might as well ask the question whether a man had the right to differ honestly with the Almighty."(4)

These unqualified and rather startling assertions afford less grounds for astonishment when the fact is remembered that they imply the acceptance of another doctrine quite as unusual as the one involved. This basic principle is that the President of the church is "the very mouthpiece of God"; "His vicegerent on earth," and the sole channel through which He communicates

His will and purposes concerning all that pertains to His kingdom on earth.

If illustrations of the practical workings of the power of the priesthood are desired, they are easily to be found and their meaning appears to be perfectly clear.

Brigham Young revised and institutionalized Joseph Smith's temple ceremonies beginning in late 1845 in Nauvoo. Note the Masonic square and compass pin on his shirt.

The Mysteries of Godliness, p.131(c)

W. S. Godbe and his colleagues were cut off from the church because they presumed to deny the right of Brigham Young to restrict freedom of thought and speed, and to discipline them for opinion's sake, and because they did not accept his financial policy. Moses Thatcher held opinions concerning his rights and privileges as an American citizen which did not accord with those of the First Presidency and the other members of the quorum of Apostles, and he "declined to take counsel." For this he was ousted from his position as an Apostle, and disfellowshipped. Charles A. Smurthwaite felt that the President of the church should not enter the commercial field in competition with persons less highly placed, and he gave voice to this opinion to his Bishop and was cut off from the church. B. H. Roberts, noting an unmistakable

partiality in the application of a church rule in the interest of one political party and against the other, entered politics without the approval of the church authorities, and was made to feel the sting of their displeasure, but later was "reconciled" with his brethren.(6)

B. H. Roberts who is, perhaps, the brainiest man in the church, as he is the most independent thinker, the most prolific writer, and possibly, the fairest controversialist, recently gave frank expression, in a: conference address, to his belief that the Mormon people had not always been blameless in the things they had done; that their conduct had not always been defensible; that "there was much of fanaticism, much of narrowness, and bigotry, and unwisdom on the part of individuals among the Latter Day Saints;" that the disasters which overtook the followers of the prophet in Missouri were due, in part at least, to boastfulness, over-zeal, fanaticism and unwisdom on the part of the people. Even the Prophet, Joseph Smith, the speaker pointed out, made mistakes, for which the Lord rebuked him. In these statements there would seem to be nothing deserving rebuke, yet for this frank avowal of facts, of the truth of which his historical studies had convinced him, he was taken sharply to task in the same session of the conference by the President of the church,

Joseph F. Smith.(7) Such results as are here indicated, need occasion no surprise, for it must be remembered, as already remarked, that the authorities, the Priesthood, are "in very deed a part of God," and as such they can fix, irrevocably, the ultimate status of man, for to them belongs the power "to bind on earth that which shall be bound in heaven and to loose on earth that which shall be loosed in heaven;" "to remit sin;" "to say what shall be done and how it shall be done and on what occasions it shall be done," and when the President of the church speaks "anything as the mind and will of the Lord, it is just as binding upon us as if God spoke personally to us."(8)

Those who are acquainted with the teachings and literature of the Mormon church need no proof to convince them that obedience to the Priesthood on the part of adherents of this faith, is one of the fundamental requirements, now, as it always has been. As already pointed out, denial of this principle was one of the chief offenses of those who were responsible for the "Utah Schism." "It had been argued that we must passively and uninquiringly obey the Priesthood

because otherwise we could riot build up Zion," complained 1;. L. T. Harrison, iii "An Appeal to the People and Protest." And such obedience appears to lie required iii all the relations of life-iii things spiritual and temporal.(9)

Some of us who are unacquainted with the refinements, modifications, or qualifications to which such teachings may be subjected in their application to individual cases may well be pardoned if we question whether a member of an organization which makes such demands upon its votaries-demands so unusual, far-reaching and seemingly opposed to freedom of

action--is in any position to act freely, as our teachings require. And if he is not really free: if because of a primary allegiance such as that involved in the doctrines we leave been considering, another could command. instant and implicit obedience in all the concerns of life could one so circumstanced be considered good material for our Rites?

We are not unmindful of the fact that leaders of the Latter Day Saints' organization leave insisted, arid do insist, that their members are as free to choose their course, to follow their preferences in all the affairs of life, as are the disciples of any other faith or philosophy of life. The reconciliation of such assertions with unquestioned facts does not lie within the field of our present undertaking. But, when issues the most vital, having to do with time and eternity, are made to hinge upon acceptance of the fundamental principle of obedience to a priesthood, then we freely confess that such assertions make an unwarranted and impossible demand upon our stock of credulity.

(1) Proceedings Grand Lodge Nevada, 1866, pp. 28-53 ; Grand Lodge of Utah, 1872, p. 15 ; 1882, pp. 22, 28, 78 ; 1883, pp. 16, 24; 104 ; 1880, p. 18 ; 1884,. pp. 75-76, 79, 92 ; 1877, p. 11; 1879, p. 29, and many others. For more recent expressions see Proceedings Utah, 1923, pp. 65-66; 1924, pp. 25, 56-58, 59, 81, 82.

(2) Smoot Investigation, vol. IV, pp. 343, 344, 345, 346, 487-88.

(3) 68th Semi-Annual Conference Report, pp. 6, 71; 83rd Annual Conference Report, p. 37. Illustrations of this abound. Said Joseph F. Smith, late President of the church: "When a man says you may direct me spiritually but not temporally, lie lies in the presence of God." Deseret News, April 25, 1895, see also same paper, December 6th, 1900. See, The Latter Day Saints, Kauffman, pp. 81f ; cf. Smoot Investigation, vol. 111, pp. 274-277.

(4) *Tullidge's Quarterly Magazine*, vol. I, p. 33. On the general subject of obedience to the priesthood, see George Q. Cannon, Contributor, vol. XXIX, p. 745 ; Smoot Investigation, vol. IV, p. 414; *Gospel Doctrine*, Josepli F. Smith, quoting *Journal of Discourses*, vol. XXIV, p. 187, 194.

(5) Manual Mutual Improvement Association 1901-02, pp. 8182; 69th Annual Conference Report, pp. 5, 6, 7; 70th Annual Conference Report, p. 52;

Outlines of Ecclesiastical History, Roberts, p. 368; Thatcher Episode (B. Young Jr.) p. 14; *Salt Lake Tribune*, April 4, 1921; Smoot Investigation vol. IV, p. 81, 414, 416; 72nd Semi-Annual Conference Report, p. 2; 75th Semi-Annual Conference Report, p. 5, and many other references; 68th Annual Conference Report, pp. 68, 69; *Improvement Era*, vol. IV, p. 230; vol. VI, p, 180; *Gospel Doctrine*, Joseph F. Smith, p. 45.

(6) *Tullidge's Quarterly Magazine*, vol. 1, p. 32; Thatcher Episode, p. 19, 35, compare pages 29-31; Smoot Investigation, Vol IV, pp. 78-81; vol. I, pp. 723, 1012 ; Supplement to Gospel Problems, Bennion, pp. 81-82.

(7) Mt. Meadow Massacre, Gibbs, p. 5; 80th Semi-Annual Conference Report, pp. 103-104, 124, 125; Gospel Doctrine, Joseph F. Smith, p. 223; Smoot Investigation, vol. III, pp. 274, 275, 276-277.

(8) 70th Annual Conference Report, p. 12; 72nd Semi-Annual Conference Report, p. 2; 75th Semi-Annual Conference Report, p. 5; 69th Annual Conference Report, p. 17; Cf. Deseret News, Oct. 4, 1896 ; *Journal of Discourses*, vol. XXIV, pp. 187-194, quoted in Gospel Doctrine, p. 56; 83rd Annual Conference Report, p. 37.

(9) Smoot Investigation, vol. IV, p. 348 ; 70th Annual Conference Report, p. 13; 68th Semi-

Annual Conference Report, p. 71; Tullidge's Quarterly Magazine, vol. 1, pp. 32, 33; Journal of Discourses, vol. 12, p. 59; vol. 5, p. 100, 187; vol. VI, p. 345; An Epistle to the Presidents, etc. John Taylor, 1882, pp. 7, 8, 9, 10; Inside of Mormonism, McMillan, p. 67; Doctrine and Covenants, Section 12-1; Deseret News, April 25, 1895: Logan Journal, May 26, 1898; Improvement Era, vol. VIII, pp. 620, 623. Said President Wilford Woodruff: "I prophesy in the name of Israel's God the day has come when the mouths of Wilford Woodruff, George Q. Cannon, Joseph F. Smith and these twelve Apostles . should not be closed because of the opinions of the children of men. There have been feelings that these men . .. .. . should say nothing about politics... My mouth shall not be closed upon these principles. I know it is the duty of the Latter Day Saints to unite together in your local affairs, the election of your city councils, the election of men to act for you in the affairs of state   And this idea of a person being afraid of somebody because he is a Democrat or a Republican, it is all wrong. I feel like saying to you, as the President of this Church, and do state, that it is your duty to unite together and appoint good men to act in every capacity for the public welfare." 68th Semi-Annual Conference Report, p. 71.

CHAPTER X

Other significant facts and teachings; polygamy in Mormon books o f instruction, literature, and teaching; "living one's religion;" influence of leaders.

Another set of facts which cannot well be ignored in this study has to do with the subject of polygamy. The writer appreciates the fact that by many this is set down as a dead issue, and that others, not n few, deprecate ally reference to the matter. He is also mindful of the fact that the President of the Church, back in 1890, issued a Manifesto, in which. he advised the people that he proposed to obey the law, and to use his influence to induce them to do the same. And further, that later, this famous document was construed as prohibiting not only new plural marriages, but also a continuance of the old relations.(1) Nor is the significance of a recent incident overlooked, wherein the present head of the church-Heber J. Grant-declared, with so much earnestness that he afterwards apologized for the manner in which he had spoken, having been, as he expressed himself, "gloriously mad," that "No man on earth has power to perform plural marriages," and, "We have excommunicated two patriarchs who have pretended to perform plural marriages." (2)

All of this and these, for reasons that follow, do not remove the subject beyond the -purview of the Mason, or of the Lodge, that may be seeking information concerning the fitness of applicants for admission into the Fraternity. To be sure, and for reasons that are obvious, the matter under consideration does not have the interest or bulk as large as it did when Grand Secretary Diehl, in compliance with resolutions adopted by Grand Lodge, prepared and sent out his Circular on Mormonism and Masonry some forty years ago(3). But after all allowances have been made with reference to this subject there still remain considerations pertinent to the purpose of this study, at all events, such is the conviction of the present writer. He is not convinced that this is a "dead issue," for he remembers that a president of the church, the "very mouthpiece of God," as we have been repeatedly assured, in the most solemn manner and without any qualification, declared concerning the doctrine and practice of polygamy: "it is one of the most vital parts of our religious faith; it emanated from God and cannot be legislated away ....take this from us and you rob us of our hopes and associations in the resurrection."(4)

And a later president of the church in his statement to the court, before receiving sentence for violation of Federal law, declared. "Though I go to prison, God will not change His law of celestial marriage."(5)

The uninitiated may experience some difficulty, perhaps, when they undertake to reconcile one set of facts with another set of facts that appear to be at opposite poles. That, however, is not a part of our problem; with the facts which follow, though, we are concerned. Here is the situation:

It is known that the practice of polygamy has been abandoned, according to repeated statements to that effect by those who are in authority, and that the principle, or doctrine, is no longer taught by the church: And yet, there are certain facts and conditions which are bound to prove troublesome to any one who would take such assertions at their face value. For example, it is a matter of common knowledge that the present head of the Mormon church is a polygamist, as also was his immediate predecessor, and as were all those who have occupied that position before him. Associated with him are other leaders similarly situated as to marital relations. These men are molders of the thought and exemplars of the principles of the organization, and they are "living their religion."(6)

This matter is not referred to here in any unkindly or carping spirit of criticism, but for the purpose of directing attention to the teaching value of such facts. "Your actions speak so loud that I cannot hear what you say," is an adage that is not without suggestiveness in this connection. "How more forcibly could you teach it (polygamy) than by practicing it openly as the head of the church," was a question asked President Joseph F. Smith, at Washington, for which he seemed to have no adequate answer.(7) Now, unquestionably the influence of the First Presidency, more particularly of the President of the church, is greater, more potent and far-reaching than that exerted by any other man or set of men. How can it be otherwise, all personal considerations aside, in view of the fact-as accepted by Latter Day Saints-that he is the very mouthpiece of the Almighty, and that God does actually speak through his lips? Necessarily it must follow that the words, the actions, the daily life of one vested with such singular prerogatives exert an influence not to be measured by any ordinary standards. It reaches the springs of action, silently but surely shapes opinion and belief, and goes far, very far, in determining the attitude of many thousands toward the institutions and the laws of the country.(8)

For a man, or for men, so placed to hold and to teach for any considerable length of time, that a law with which they do not find themselves in agreement, is unconstitutional and therefore should be ignored and this in spite of the fact that the highest tribunal in the land had declared such law to be consistent with the constitution; (9) or for them to insist that the practice of polygamy "is ordained of God . . . . . . is ecclesiastical in its nature and government," and because this is so, "it is therefore outside of constitutional law," and hence "being within the pale of the church, its free exercise cannot be prohibited;" or, again, for the "vicegerent of God" to testify in the most conspicuous manner (though not of his own free will) that he had been, was then, and expected to continue living in known violation of the laws of his country, his church, and his God, and was willing to take his chances with the laws of his state; and for other leaders, only a little less prominent, to testify to similar conditions in their marital relations and to the possession of a like purpose with regard to the law-for such a situation to develop, and to exist for years, and to be taken quite as a matter of course, or even approved and commended and rewarded by such a considerable body of people, cannot but be productive of results that are far from being reassuring.(10)

How can it be otherwise than that this attitude toward law, and these examples of the most influential men in the church, should have a far-reaching effect upon the young men and women of the Latter Day Saints' organization? As Masons, and as citizens, we hold that it is not desirable, certainly it is not in accord with Masonic ideals and teachings, to subject young people to character-forming influences which must tend, at least, to make them indifferent to the basic law of our country." Many thoughtful Craftsmen are profoundly convinced that these are times in which unhesitating and unequivocating regard for law should be emphasized on all suitable occasions, and that the all too general practice, in effect, of nullifying and repealing law by disregard of law, in place of making use of the means provided by law, is a proceeding dangerous beyond calculation; it is a positive, subtle menace threatening the very foundations of those institutions of which we boast and in which we glory.

Another angle of this phase of the subject must not be neglected. Hardly less pertinent than the matter just discussed is the fact that this principle, like the revelation which established it, continues to hold its place in the teachings, the beliefs and the literature of the Mormon people. Not only is this doctrine taught by example, and that by the most influential men in the church, but it appears in the instructional and other literature provided by the church, or issued with its approval, and in verbal instructions and testimony given at various gatherings of the people.(12)

The Doctrine and Covenants is one of the four standard works adopted by formal action of the Church. It is the word of God, and is of equal authority with the Bible, the Book of Mormon, and the Pearl of Great Price-these being the four standard books of the Latter Day Saints' organization. In section, or chapter 132 of this book is the revelation on plural marriage. If that chapter ever taught this principle -and there is no controversy on that point-it still teaches it, for the late President of the church, Joseph F. Smith, testified under oath that it had not been annulled or repealed, and so far. as known to the present writer, no action of this sort has been taken, or contemplated; it is still part and parcel of the authoritative teachings of the church, as also is the severe sentence which it pronounces upon those who fail to accept this teaching.(13)

In the material provided for study in the young people's organizations of the church considerable stress is placed on the "Lives" of Joseph and Hyrum Smith, Brigham Young, John Taylor and other leaders in the history of this people, all of whom "lived their religion," and suffered "persecution," when the Government sought to have its laws obeyed. These men are presented as heroic characters, whose words and example are given for instruction and emulation.(14)

Not infrequently speakers, when addressing large numbers of this faith, declare their adherence to the principle under consideration, and condemn the Government for suppressing it. Several years after the Manifesto was issued an Apostle declared that the principle of plural marriage is as true today as it ever was, and that those "who prevent you from obeying are responsible to God for so doing."(15) B. H. Roberts, in a church periodical published for the guidance and instruction of young people-members of the Mutual Improvement Associations-has a long article in explanation and defense of this principle (16).

Other illustrations of the matter under consideration could easily be assembled, but they are not deemed necessary. Enough has been said, it would seem, to make clear what is being done along this line. It is no part of the present undertaking to harmonize the contradictions which must be apparent to every observant Craftsman. The purpose here is to call attention to facts.

As these pages are written primarily for the benefit of Utah Masonry-though the subject is one that concerns Masons throughout the land-there is another point of view that should be introduced here.

The statement is sometimes made concerning one who has applied, or is desirous of applying, for the degrees: "He does not practice polygamy; never has done so, and though a member of the Mormon church he never has accepted it even in principle. Why is not he good material for the mysteries of Masonry?" Such a statement of facts would seem to leave but one answer possible, to that question, and yet, just here is a very important consideration that is usually ignored or overlooked by those who have given little thought to this subject.

There is a principle in law which exactly illustrates the point to be emphasized here. Perhaps no statement of this is better suited to the present purpose than that to be found in the Report of the Committee on Privileges and Elections in the Smoot case.

At the beginning of his argument on one of the subheads of the report, the Chairman said: "That one may be legally, as well as morally, responsible for unlawful acts which he does not himself commit is a rule of law too elementary to require discussion." Then in the concluding paragraph he restates the principle in these words:

"The rule in civil cases is the same as that which obtains in the administration of criminal law. One who is a member of an association of any nature is bound by the action of his associates, whether he favors or disapproves of such action. He can at any time protect himself from the consequences of any future action of his associates by withdrawing from the association, but while he remains a member of the association he is responsible for whatever his associates may do."(17)

Other illustrations might be given, but none that would more clearly represent the writer's view of the problem presented by the man who would retain membership in the organization and yet be absolved from certain of its teachings and practices. The second sentence in the quotation above suggests the proper and the only honorable course under the circumstances indicated.(18)

(1) The Manifesto has been printed many times, in pamphlet form and as a part of other works. It is included in the 1914 edition of Doctrine and Covenants, not, we think, earlier. President Joseph F. Smith testified that its absence from that vol. of revelations was due to an oversight. Smoot Investigation, vol. I, pp. 291, 336. The document itself is to be found in the vol. just referred to, pp. 340-341; also in Reminiscences of Early Utah, Baskin, p. 243. For an interesting discussion of the Manifesto, see Smoot Investigation, vat. I, pp. 330-337. See Supplement, Gospel Problems, Bennion, pp. 62, 64, 87, 88, for views of the Manifesto of one who advocates and practices polygamy, and who insists that the Manifesto was a "political declaration," and that it could not nullify a

revelation from God. Baskin in Reminiscences of Early Utah gives interesting details of events which forced "the hand of the Lord," pp. 185-186. On this subject see remarkable statement by Apostle

Penrose, *Deseret News*, July 13, 1899, in which he refers to testimony of Woodruff and Lorenzo Snow, as the personal opinions of two venerable citizens

(2) *Salt Lake Tribune*, April 5th, 1921. Cf. 91st Annual Conference Report, pp. 201-202.

(3) Proceedings Grand Lodge of Utah, 1882, p. 53; 1883, pp. 24-26.

(4) President John Taylor, *Tullidge's Quarterly Magazine*, vol. II, pp. 7, 8.

(5) Lorenzo Snow, *History of Utah*, Whitney, vol. III, p. 471. The words quoted were in answer to a statement by the prosecuting attorney, in his plea before the jury, that if the jury would convict Snow, lie (the attorney) "would predict that a new revelation would soon follow, changing the Divine law of celestial marriage:" With this compare Schuyler Colfax's Journal in *The Western Galaxy*, vol. I, p. 24.7, and Gospel Problems, Bennion, p. 44, and Supplement to Gospel Problems, Bennion, pp. 80, 87, 88.

(6) Smoot Investigation, vol. I, p. 712; compare pp. 334, 336.

(7) The question in the text was asked by Senator Burrows, Chairman of the Committee, Smoot Investigation, vol. I, p. 336; vol. IV, p. 481, also cf. vol. I, p. 195, question by Senator Hoar.

(8) Smoot Investigation, vol. III, pp. 603-605 ; compare vol. I, p. 336. With the foregoing references, compare the words of a former Mormon Bishop M'Guffie: " ....the man that is placed between God and the people, that is the law." The Latter Day Saints, Kauffman, p. 81.

(9) An Epistle of the First Presidency, etc., 1886, entire; An Epistle of the Twelve Apostles, etc., October 1.0, 1887, p. 4; *The Mormon Problem*, quoting opinion of Supreme Court of U. S., p. 70; Smoot Investigation, vol. III, p. 604; *Blood Atonement*, C. W. Penrose, p. 31.

(10) Handbook of Reference, A. H. Cannon, p. 102; Smoot Investigation, Vol. I, p. 334 (Joseph F. Smith) ; 430 (F. M. Lyman) ; 718 (B. H. Roberts) ; compare journal of Discourses, Vol. V, pp. 1-38, 100; Inside of Mormonism, pp. ?9-80; Deseret News, Jan. 16, 1889; Smoot Investigation, Vol. IV, p. 481. Says one who is a polygamist, and who believes the Manifesto was worse than a mistake: "Many of us have entered this principle since the Manifesto, and many of the leaders, living openly in this principle, are being sustained in high

positions of responsibility in the church .. . ." *Gospel Problems,* Bennion, p. 44.

(11) Smoot Investigation, vol. I, p. 336; III, pp. 603-605; IV, p. 481.

(12) Sunday School Outlines, Series B, Theological Department, Third Year, pp. 37f ; Fourth Year, pp 49-52; In these references, attention is directed to the penalties attached to failure to obey this law when it has been made known; *Young Woman's Journal*, July 1910, p. 405. Joseph F. Smith, when addressing the Weber Stake Conference, at o-,den, said, of the principle of polygamy that it was "revealed to Joseph Smith by God, and the Latter-Day Saint who denies and rejects that truth in his heart might as well reject every other truth connected with his mission." Deseret News, June 25, 1903. See also Smoot Investigation, vol. I, p. 192, also p. 193. In the Congressional Report on the Statehood Bill for Utah, May 1894, and which was favorable, these words occur, as affording one reason for granting the petition: "The Mormon Church, through all its officials, publicly, privately, and in every way possible for mortals to do and proclaim, have with bowed heads, if not in anguish, pledged their faith and honour that never more in the future shall polygamy be in the Mormon Church either a doctrine of faith or practice." In

connec. tion with this quotation, see *Gospel Problems*, Bennion, p. 44.

(13) Smoot Investigation, vol I, p. 108. Several years after his fattier testified as indicated in the text, Apostle Hyrum Smith, at an annual Conference of the church, and in the presence of his father, declared: "These revelations are written in the Doctrine and Covenants, Book of Mormon and Pearl of Great Price. * * * They were proclaimed by revelation as I have stated, and up to this time, after over seventy-seven years of existence of the Church, not one principle or doctrine thus revealed has been receded from by the members of the Church. We have never repudiated any of the truths revealed to the Prophet Joseph Smith and to his successors in the office of Prophet, Seer and Revelator to the church of Jesus Christ of Latter-Day Saints. We have never relinquished our belief in any one of these doctrines and principles. * * * We have never been called upon or found it necessary in any stage of our progress to eliminate any revelation from the record. Neither have we ever denied any of them. We testify in all soberness that these revelations are from God. They are therefore the same yesterday, today and for ever, and are everlasting and essential to the salvation of those unto whom they are given." Seventy-eighth Annual Conference

Report, 1907, p. 31. Apostle Mathias F. Cowley, in an address before a Quarterly Conference, Logan, said: "None of these revelations of the prophets either past or present have been repealed . . . . . . These revelations received by our prophets and seers are all of God, and we cannot repeal or disannul them without making God out a liar and God cannot lie." See Protest of Citizens, p. 20. Compare Lorenzo Snow, ante p. 37; *Historical Record*, vol. VI, p. 144.

(14) 87th Annual Conference Report pp. 6, 7. See also Historical Record vol. VI p. 145 for account of release of ' Lorenzo Snow from the Utah Penitentiary.

(15) *Salt Lake Herald*, April 5, 1918, two thousand people said to have been present. *Logan Journal*, January 29, 1898.

(16) *Improvement Era*, vol. I, pp. 472, 475, 478, 482.

(17) Smoot Investigation, vol. III, p. 608; IV, pp. 454, 485, 486.

(18) In the discussion of the matter quoted the fact is brought out, in connection with the Haymarket Riots, Chicago, 1893, "that the anarchists were not convicted upon the ground that they had participated in the murder of which they were

convicted .. . . They were convicted because they belonged to an organization which, as an organization, advised the commission of acts which would lead to murder: Smoot Investigation, vol. IV, p. 485.

CHAPTER XI

Place of "belief" in Masonry; illustrated in naturalization laws; the Great Light and "living oracles"; the Deity; many gods, including female deity; attitude of Mormon church toward Masonry.

THE unthinking Craftsman, and sometimes those who are in a position to know, find a stumbling block in the fact that a Grand Lodge does, or should, consider the matter of "belief," in connection with qualifications of applicants for the degrees, for membership by affiliation, or for the privilege of visitation. Attention will be directed to certain facts presently which-in addition to those set forth in the preceding pages-may help to a more nearly correct appreciation of the actual situation in Utah, and of the principles which through the years have determined, and do now determine, the position of the Grand Lodge of the Beehive state. But first, it is quite worth our while to take a little nearer view of a claim often made in behalf of Masonry, but which like many another assertion that comes, presumably, from authoritative sources, should be received with a due amount of caution.

The impression quite generally prevails that Masonry does not presume to question a petitioner concerning his belief, or religion. "He may believe what he pleases," so the Craft is informed by those who have given the matter hardly a second thought, "so long as lie accepts the one Masonic dogma, of the existence of God, the Great

Architect of the Universe." But is that true? Do Grand Lodges stop with that? Is there one Grand Lodge, at least in Anglo-Saxon countries, that is content to take as it stands, Article 1 of the "Charges of a Freemason," for example, and abide by the definition of "religion," found therein? Hardly. The creed-maker must needs come forward with his pet target!(1)

To point out the fallaciousness of the assumption under consideration may seem to be a work of supererogation, but there may be some readers of this, who have been misled by oft-repeated declarations. " Significant testimony relating to the matter in hand will be drawn from two sources. First, from records. Space permits only the briefest references.

Here is a great eastern jurisdiction, with more than 100,000 members on its rosters, laying down in its Constitution as an essential part of the foundation of its Masonic edifice, the dogma of Monotheism in connection

with belief in Deity.(2) As will be seen from later paragraphs in this study, that one word has a very direct bearing on the Utah situation, and would ,exclude Latter Day Saints from Masonic affiliation in the jurisdiction referred to.

Down along the Mexican border is another great jurisdiction-great in many respects-which has placed in its Code the requirement, that must be met by all applicants, of "a belief in the Divine authenticity of the Holy Bible."(3)

Eastward, but still in the most southern tier of states, is another jurisdiction which has adopted a "Declaration of Masonic Faith as to God and the Holy Bible" and has nailed it down by requiring that it shall be read in each lodge, that it shall be spread upon the minute-book, and that report that this has been done shall be made to the Grand secretary by the secretary of the lodge, and further, that this "Declaration" shall be printed in the next Manual.(4) And yet, that creed contains no less than five distinct, qualifying, dogmatic, doctrinal statements with reference to Deity. Turning East again, we hear a Grand Master declare in his annual address "Our Book of Constitutions teaches us that that Sublime Person, the Lion of the Tribe of Judah, is Christ, the Son of the Living God; and if our Book of Constitutions does not so teach, then is our Masonry a sounding brass and a tinkling cymbal"; and a Grand Orator of the same jurisdiction asserted that. "True Masonry...... recognizes the church as having been founded by God, with his Son Jesus Christ as the Chief cornerstone."(5) Illustrations such as these could be greatly multiplied, did space permit, or the occasion require them.

The other line of evidence is to be found in the ritual, lectures and ceremonies of Masonry. For obvious reasons this cannot be presented here. But one cannot follow a candidate through the work of the several degrees, from the first question that is asked till the work is completed, and note the explicit teachings touching religion, and scarcely less definite implications and inferences, and have much room for doubt that Masonry does make very considerable demands in this respect. Masonry does claim, and exercise, the right to insist that the candidate shall profess belief in certain principles. Failing to meet this condition, and his petition would not even be presented to the lodge, to say nothing of proceeding with the work. The fact is no less apparent that the range of inquiry within which the search for information concerning an applicant may be prosecuted, is not fixed by any "immutable landmarks," for the law on "qualifications" varies greatly in the different jurisdictions. Masonry has erected certain standards to which applicants must conform; it does pass on qualifications; necessarily, too, it must, and does, rate character, and in order to judge character, somewhat must be known concerning the stuff that has gone into the making of character. And so it comes about that when the desired information is not at hand, many questions are asked, or should be asked, which do not find place on the forms of petition. Circumstances might be such that members of an investigation committee would desire to satisfy themselves whether or not an applicant for initiation is a drug addict, or a user, or maker of intoxicants, or a "libertine"; whether he abuses his wife, neglects his children, defrauds his creditors, or is wedded to the gaming-table. And it is within the province of this committee to make enquiries with reference to the physical condition of a petitioner; whether he is a cripple, or subject to any chronic or other disease which might lessen his efficiency, or cause him to be a burden to the lodge. All these intimate matters of health, moral qualities, business, social and domestic relations of a candidate are of vital concern to the lodge, and upon them it should be fully advised.

Now, to maintain that the most powerful of all character-shaping forces should be excluded from the field of inquiry, and that' no standard may be erected by which the religious bearing of a life may be calculated--that these are matters of indifference to a Masonic Lodge, or, if you please, "none of its business"-is an absurdity, in the opinion of the present writer. Certainly, such a contention does not conform to facts or to practice. The statement may not be necessary, and the writer's fear of being misunderstood may be groundless, but he would remind his readers that in dealing with this phase of the subject, he has in mind, always, *religion* not *sectarianism.*

In this connection, and as further emphasizing the importance that may be attached to a state of mind, to a "belief," as a determining factor in the evaluation of character, the decision of a Salt Lake Judge, in the Third District Court, is illuminating and suggestive. The matter came up on the petition of an alien to become a citizen of the United States.

In framing the naturalization laws under the statute certain requirements are set-forth. Failure to satisfy any one of these conditions results in defeating application for citizenship. Among other declarations required the petitioner must state under oath that he is not "a polygamist or believer in the practice of polygamy." And further, he must make it "appear to the satisfaction of the court," that he is attached to the principles of the Constitution of the United States.(6) In the case under consideration the applicant for citizenship took oath as required, with reference to being a polygamist and his belief in the practice of polygamy. At the hearing, however, he was interrogated with respect to fulfillment of conditions required for admission to citizenship. The testimony showed, with reference to belief in the practice of polygamy, that the petitioner based his disbelief in the practice upon the conviction, and upon no other ground, that so long as they exist, the prohibitory rules of. church and state should be obeyed. He did not disbelieve in it because of any objection to the practice itself: "* * * * apart from its relationship to ecclesiastical and legal prohibitions he does believe in it now." He was willing to obey the law, and to have it obeyed, but it was shown that he did not believe in, and was unsympathetic with, the forbidding canons of both church and state. The Court held that "One cannot honestly believe in a practice apart from the fact that it is against the law, and at the same time be honestly attached to the law forbidding it." And further that "* * * since his testimony shows a lack of attachment to the law against polygamy, a law fundamental in our scheme of government, he has failed to fulfill that important condition requiring petitioners to show to the satisfaction of the court that they are `attached to the principles of the constitution.' "(7) Admission to citizenship. was therefore denied him.

The point to which attention is specially directed in this incident is the significance attached to a "belief," as disclosing an unfavorable attitude of mind toward the laws of the lard. Masonry, like citizenship acquired through naturalization, is a privilege, not a right, and a privilege conditioned upon compliance with certain requirements, and those requirements are fixed by the written and unwritten laws of the Fraternity.

Another matter, not without significance in this connection, concerns the Book of the Law. Masonry directs the attention of its initiates to the Bible, "the inestimable gift from God to man as the rule and guide to his faith and conduct." The Great Light, in Anglo-Saxon Masonry, occupies a prominent and well known position in the Ritual and Lodge room. For these reasons the attitude of the Latter Day Saints' organization towards this "moral manual of civilization" is of no small significance.

The Bible is accepted as the "Word of God, so far as translated correctly."(9) The Book of Mormon is equally the word of God, as also are the Doctrine and Covenants and the Pearl of Great Price-these are the standard books of the Mormon church.(10)

In this respect, then, there would seem to be little ground for objection, for with four bibles surely, a Book of the Law could be placed upon the altar, axed if not one, then two; or three, or all four. But there is another angle to this feature of the subject.

Among the many doctrines, or principles, held by the Mormon church-and in this instance, given place among its fundamental teachings, is that of continuous, or "immediate revelation." By this is understood that the President of the church, who, as we have seen, is the "very mouthpiece of God,"(11) may at any time

substitute something better than any one of the four books named, or than all of them together, and such pronouncement would be the very word of God, binding alike upon all the adherents of that faith. "The whole of them, (i. e. the four books listed above) are not all we need * * * the Lord has his `mouthpiece to say what shall be done and how it shall be done and on what occasion it shall be done.' "(12) The authorities of the church are the "living oracles of God and they are word pore to the L. D. S. than all the Bibles, all the Books of Mormon and all the Books of Doctrine and Covenants that are written. If we could have but one of them, give me the living oracles of the Priesthood for my guidance."(13) "When compared with the living oracles," declared Brigham Young, "those books are nothing to me; those books do not convey the word of God direct to us now, as do the words of the Prophet or a man bearing the Holy Priesthood in our day and generation. I would rather have the living oracles than all the writing in the books." These words, quoted by President Woodruff, were spoken in the presence of Joseph Smith, who immediately arose and said: "Brother Brigham has told you the word of the Lord and he has told you the truth."(14)

Attention is directed to these teachings, not in any captious spirit, nor in criticism of those who hold these views.

Such instructions, more especially those touching the relative importance of the Bible and the "living oracles" of the Mormon church, are for those who can, and who care to, accept them. The paint emphasized here is that such views do concern Masons-wherever Masons are to be found-when those who hold them seek the fraternal fellowship and the more intimate relations of Lodge membership. Freemasons can hardly look unmoved, or with any measure of favor, upon the application of one who seeks the benefits and privileges of the Craft, and who yet, at any moment, because of conscientious scruples, might turn from the Great Light of Masonry, substituting for the "inestimable gift from God to man," the dictum of some man whom accident has lifted to a place of great influence, but in whose pronouncements Masonry finds no marks of divine authority. That this may not appear in the light of a mere suppositious case, or a vastly removed possibility, the reader's attention is invited to the paragraphs dealing with the attitude of the Mormon church toward secret societies.(15) As will be seen by reference to that passage, a late "living oracle" declared secret societies-and the connection shows that Masonry was included-are of the "evil one," and the same authoritative voice asserted that the church had passed a resolution that Latter Day Saints who were members of secret societies were not fit for offices in the church or positions of responsibility. This latter fact leas a further significance in that it indicates that such applicants as are being considered here, are not free to choose such course as might appeal to them, as was brought out in an earlier passage: pressure, of the character indicated above makes freedom of action impossible, for honors and dignities in the church are among the strongest incentives to loyalty to the organization.

In view of such facts as are here set forth: with "living oracles" whose words may at any time supersede the rule and guide of the Mason's faith and practice, and with fairly definite information as to the character of such pronouncements, where Masonry might be concerned- members of the Craft may be pardoned, perhaps, for exercising a large measure of caution when the petition of a Latter Day Saint is presented. And the necessity for this course is not lessened by the fact that two of the four standard works or bibles of the Mormon church condemn in unsparing and unmistakable terms, all secret organizations.(16)

Another aspect of the subject in hand which is worthy of more than passing notice relates itself to Deity. Masonry requires of its initiates an avowal of belief in Deity. It does not undertake to prescribe what one's conception shall be,(17) so that in this particular, Latter Day Saints would seem to be qualified to meet requirements. But these facts do not preclude a consideration of conceptions so fundamental in character and life as one's apprehension of Deity. Speaking in a general way, according as one's idea of God is exalted or otherwise, will the ideals be lofty or debased. (18)

Here, again, the writer would disclaim any intention or attempt to criticize those whose views are under consideration. The chief object in view is to present as much information as possible concerning the influences and forces and beliefs which operate together in the task of shaping the character of adherents of the system, some aspects of which are here being passed under review.

Latter Day Saints are taught, and, we assume believe, in a plurality of gods. "When I lave preached on the subject of Deity, it has been the plurality of Gods."(19) "The head God organized the heavens. In the beginning the heads of the Gods organized the heavens and the earth." "In the beginning the Bible shows there is a plurality of Gods beyond the power of refutation." "The head of the Gods appointed one God for us."(20) "Jesus Christ and His Father are two distinct persons, in the same sense as John and Peter are two persons." "Each of these Gods, including Jesus Christ and His Father . . . . . . is subject to the laws which govern, ot necessity, even the most refined order of physical existence."(21)

Further, not only is the doctrine of plurality of gods taught, and believed, by the Mormon people, but the materiality of the gods as well. A statement with slight variations often heard in Utah is: "God Himself was once as we are now, and is an exalted man, and sits enthroned in yonder heavens."(22) This doctrine " . . . . . .affirms that God the Father, as well as God the Son, is a corporeal personage; that he has a body of flesh and bones; that he has form, and dimensions, organs and parts as to his body .. . . . ."(23) ". . . . . . the principle of procreation. By it, and through that principle the worlds are peopled ..... God possesses it, and we as His children inherit that power."(24) "Jesus Christ and His Father are two persons . . . . . . Each of them has an organized, individual tabernacle, embodied in material form, and composed of material substance; in the likeness of man, and possessing every organ, limb and physical part that man possesses."(25) "What is God? He is a material intelligence, possessing both body and parts. He is in the form of man, and is in fact of the same species; . . . . . . He can go, come, converse, reason, eat, drink, love, hate, rejoice, possess and enjoy ...." (26) Associated with this God, who "sits enthroned in yonder heaven," is a female Deity. By this arrangement provision appears to be made for the pre-existence of spirits. These spirits possess "every organ after the pattern and in the likeness or similitude of the outward or fleshly tabernacle they are destined eventually to inhabit . . . . . . This individual, spiritual body, was begotten by the Heavenly Father, in His own likeness and image, and by the laws of procreation."(27)

Whatever allowance may, and should, be made, in respect to leaving every man free to conceive of God as he will, due consideration should be given to this fact, namely: The conception of God herein set forth differs so radically from that held by Masons generally, but especially in this country, that the question might well arise, whether those who accept it-and who are absolutely within their rights in doing so would, or could, fit into the Masonic institution and system. If sincere in their faith, they could hardly feel at home in an organization, some of whose fundamental teachings are so at variance with their own beliefs and ideals. And, on the other hand, Masons are fully warranted in exercising the greatest care when considering any matter which might threaten, or actually disturb, the peace and harmony of a Lodge.

Reference has been made to the unfriendly attitude of the Mormon church toward all secret societies. The reason for this opposition, according to the late President of the church, Joseph F. Smith, "must be apparent to every intelligent Latter Day. Saint."(28) The reader who does not come within this classification must look elsewhere for information on this point. As briefly as possible some of the considerations bearing on this matter will be given here, and in order to conserve space, all the references will be assembled under one numeral.

The Latter Day Saints' organization is opposed to secret societies because, among other reasons:

"They are of the evil one." Satan was the originator of secret societies, he having made Cain a "Master Mahan," so that he might slay his brother Abel and avoid punishment; revelation has condemned them; "covenants they impose are liable to conflict with religious obligations;" a prophet of God has emphatically raised his voice against these "institutions which threaten the liberties of all people and portend the destruction of whatever nation fosters them;" membership in such organizations interferes with performance of church duties, such as attending meetings of their quorums, paying tithing and going on missions; affiliation with such societies means that the Latter Day Saint forfeits his "inheritance in the Zion of God;" such membership means that the advice of the First Presidency has been ignored and disregarded; "nothing can be permitted in the members (of the church) that is calculated to bring division and weakness to the church;" those who have been led to join such societies should repent and withdraw "from that which threatens their standing;" these organizations are no place for a Latter Day Saint, for by becoming identified with them he leaves the teachings of the gospel and plays "into the hands of the Gentiles."(29) So strong is the opposition of the church to any connection with secret societies, on the part of its members, that the authorities some years ago took drastic action, going so far as to declare that those who were identified with these organizations should not be selected for any church office, for they "are not fit to hold these offices," and later, the President of the church threatened such with excommunication. (30)

Now, such being the attitude of the Latter Day Saints' church toward Masonry, the matter appears to be plain and beyond dispute that a person who would act in opposition to such counsel and to the most solemn and positive asseverations of such authorities--including the president of the church, who speaks for God to his people, and who binds on earth .and it is bound in heaven--would, necessarily, be a "bad" Mormon. And Masons may be pardoned, perhaps, should they seriously doubt if a "bad" Mormon can be made over into a good Mason.

(1) The "Charges" are referred to here, because of the position they are supposed to hold, and do hold in many jurisdictions, in Masonic thought and jurisprudence, and because Article I furnishes the basis of the claim discussed in the text. An interesting example of the devastating work of the creed-monger is to be found in the Constitutions of the United Grand Lodge of England (1896) , p. 3, where this Article is to be found, in its revamped form. The writer is not unfamiliar with the fact that the premier Grand Lodge never has accepted the "Charges of a Freemason" as "possessing any legislative authority, or as representing the laws for the government of the modern Brotherhood." Hughan, letter to Lawrence Greenleaf, Colorado, under date of Feb. 11, 1899. Utah Proceedings, 1901, Correspondence Report, pp. 15-16. The matter is

not without interest and bearing in this connection, however.

(2) Massachusetts Code, 1923, p. 4.

(3) Code of Texas, 1908, p. 186.

(4) Proceedings Alabama, 1919, quoted in full, Correspondence Report of Georgia for 1920.

(5) Proceedings West Virginia,, 1914.

(6) Naturalization Laws and Regulations, 1915, p. 5.

(7) Decision, Judge Harold M. Stephens (Mss.) 1917, pp. 2, 3, 8; cf. R. W. Young, Smoot Investigation, vol. 11, p. 968.

(8) The Builder, Newton, p. 265.

(9) Articles of Faith, Talmage, (1899) p. 240f.

(10) Smoot Investigation, vol. I, p. 179.

(11) Apostle A. O. Woodruff, 69th Annual Conference Report, pp. S, 6, 7; Apostle M. W. Merrill, same Report, p. 17.

(12) Apostle M. W. Merrill, 69th Annual Conference Report, p. 17; "Wilford Woodruff is the prophet and seer of this church . . . . . . Joseph Smith was a prophet ; Brigham Young was a prophet; Wilford Woodruff is a prophet, and I know that he has a great many prophets around

him, and he can make scriptures as good as those in the Bible." Apostle John Taylor, Annual Conference, April 5, 1897, quoted in, The Mormons and their Bible, p. 97.

(13) Apostle M. W. Merrill, 68th Semi-Annual Conference p. 6; at the same Conference, Apostle J. W. Taylor enlarged upon the same subject, taking certain of Apostle Merrill's words as a text, p. 7; for the words of President Woodruff, quoted in the teat, see same Report, pp. 22-23; cf. Y.M.M.A. Manual, 1901-1902, p. 81

(14) 68th Semi-Annual Conference Report, p. 23.

Seq15. pp. 88-90.

(16) Pearl of Great Price, 1891, pp. 14-16; Book of Mormon, 1920, 2 Nephi 9:9; 26:22; Helaman 2:2-10; 7:25-27; 8:1, 4; 3 Nephi 6:25-30; 7:6-11; Ether 8:14-25, and many other passages. See also the present writer's article on, Anti-Masonry in the Book of Mormon.

(17) The statement in the text is modified by the fact that indirectly and by implication Masonry does this very thing, beyond peradventure. To illustrate: Freemasonry lays stress upon the great principle of the brotherhood of man. Now, such a relationship necessarily strikes its roots into the greater fact of the Fatherhood of God, and

fatherhood suggests certain very definite relationships, which in turn involve attributes of Deity.

(18) A suggestive sidelight on this comes from the experience of the missionaries of the Roman Church among the Goths. Ulfilas, an outstanding figure in this work, translated the Scriptures into the Gothic language, " ....omitting from his version, however, the Books of the Kings, as he feared that the stirring recital of wars and battles in that portion of the Word might kindle into too fierce a flame the martial ardor of his new converts."

(19) Joseph Smith, the prophet, *Millenial Star*, vol. XXIII, p. 246, quoted by Roberts in his, *The Mormon Doctrine of Deity*, . p. 10. To the Mormons, the Christian conception of Deity-better, the view, for the most part held by the Christian churches-is "absurd, contradictory and unscriptural." B. H. Roberts, Improvement Era, vol. I, p. 763; 75th Semi-Annual Conference Report, p. ?3; *Gospel Doctrine*, Joseph F. Smith,

(20)p• 8° *Mormon Doctrine of Deity*, Roberts, pp. 10, 42, 231f; *Millenial Star*, vol. XXIV, p. 108.

(21) *Key to Theology*, P. P. Pratt, pp. 34, 37.

(22) *Millenial Star*, vol. 246, quoted by Roberts, in *Mormon Doctrine of Deity*, p. 10.

(23) *Improvement Era*, vol. I, Roberts, p. ?62.

(24) George Q. Cannon, 69th Annual Conference Report, p. 20.

(25) *Key to Theology*, P. P. Pratt, p. 34.

(26) P. P. Pratt, in the *Prophet*, quoted by B. H. Roberts in, *Mormon Doctrine of Deity*, p. 255; *Articles of Faith*, Talmage, quoted by B. H. Roberts, *Defense of the Faith*, vol. II, p. 268.

(27) Key to Theology, P. P. Pratt, pp. 51-52. The same thought finds expression in a favorite hymn, "Oh, my Father," much used in Mormon gatherings. It was written by Eliza R. Snow, sister of President Lorenzo Snow, and one of the plural wives of the prophet Joseph Smith, and later, of Brigham Young. One should read all the stanzas, only part of one can be given place here:

In the heavens are parents single? No; the thought makes reason stare. Truth is reason; truth eternal

Tells me I've a mother there.

    (See any L. D. S. Hymnal)

(28) *Improvement Era*, vol. IV, Joseph F. Smith, p. 59; vol. I, pp. 374-376; cf. 70th Annual Conference Report, M. W, Merrill, p. 30.

(29) Genesis 5:14-18, Joseph Smith's translation; Pearl of Great Price, pp. 14, 15, 16; Improvement Era, vol. Iv. p. 59; vol. I, p. 375, 376; Gospel Doctrine, pp. 134-136.

(30) For fear that the statements of the text may seem to be exaggerated, or be charged to prejudice of the writer, the exact words of the speaker are here reproduced. President Smith s subject was "Secret Societies." Among other things he said: "Think of the fallacies and wickedness in the people doing this. They are bound to hold secret all that transpires and to defend their members whether they are doing right or wrong .....Now, I'll tell you what the church has done about this.

We have passed a resolution that men who are identified with these secret organizations shall not be preferred as bishops, or sought for as counselors. The same when it comes to selecting M. I. A. officers. The men who have done this have disqualified themselves and are not fit to hold these offices." *Provo Enquirer*, November 12, 1900. On another occasion, when addressing a Quarterly, Conference in Provo, the same speaker took up this subject and declared that "The authorities of the church have the right, and will use it, to excommunicate members who will set aside the authority placed over them by God, for all members must act in harmony with their bishops and the stake presidency." *Provo Enquirer*, (Mormon) Jan. 13, 1902.

CHAPTER XII

CONCLUSION - SUMMARY

IN the preceding pages many matters, of varying degrees of interest and importance in connection with the subject, have been presented. Owing to the exigency of space limitations, none of these has been fully discussed, and, as a result, the study, as a whole, may give the impression of being fragmentary and incomplete. The following brief summary will assist the reader to see at a glance the ground that has been covered in the discussion, and it may serve, further, to remind him that not in the character or significance of any one consideration here set forth is to be found the object sought in these chapters, but that the cumulative weight of all the facts presented is relied upon to sustain the writer's position and contention. Expressed differently, the writer believes that the facts here assembled fully vindicate the position of the Grand Lodge of Utah, and afford ample reasons why the Masonry of Utah, and the Masonry of the entire country (for manifestly this is not, and cannot be, merely a local problem), should not open its doors to members of the Latter Day Saints' organization.(1) Now, the summary

1. *Historical*: Attitude of the Mormon Masons in Nauvoo; Grand Lodge summonses and edicts ignored; Lodge work continued after dispensation was annulled, and even after the Lodges had been declared clandestine.

2. *Clandestinism*: Temple ceremonies; use of language and symbols.

3. *Priesthood*: Claims unlimited power over members of the organization; speaks for God, and as God; binds on earth and in heaven; to question or disobey, the same as though the Almighty had commanded and had been disobeyed.

4.. *Polygamy*: Is taught,---

a. By the original revelation, which still holds its place in' the Doctrine and Covenants, and which has not been repealed or annulled, nor can it be erased.

b. By positive declarations of belief in the principle at the lips of the leaders and prominent teachers.

c. By the literature prepared for study in all the subdivisions of the system.

d. By the example of leaders, who "live their religion" today, and by the "Lives" of the leaders of other days, from Joseph Smith to the present time.

5. *Attitude Toward Law*: Enforcement of law against polygamy was "persecution;" still so held and taught; another phase illustrated by the testimony of leaders in the Smoot investigation.

6. *The Great Light*: Substitution of pronouncements of "living oracles" (specifically, of the President of the

organization) for the Bible; further, it is displaced by the Book of Mormon, as a teacher of righteousness;(2) it is *one* of the four standard books of the organization, two of which condemn secret societies in unmeasured terms, and trace their origin, particularly of Masonry, to the evil one.

7. *The Deity*: "Many gods" clearly and emphatically taught; God an "exalted man;" male and female deities; these conceptions out of harmony with teachings of Anglo-Saxon Masonry.

8. *Membership Prohibited*: Masonry originated with Satan, and because of its evil tendencies must be avoided; disregard of teachings of priesthood on this subject deprives adherents of the faith of their standing, of official preferment, and may subject them to excommunication.

The End

(1) The writer prefers the word "organization," to "church," when referring to this group, because it comprehends so much more, in principle and practice, than is generally understood when the word "church" is used.

(2) "I told the brethren that the Book of Mormon was the most correct of any book on earth, and the keystone of our religion, and a man would get nearer to God by abiding by its precepts, than by any other book." *Journal of Joseph Smith*, quoted

by B. H. Roberts in *History of the Church, Period 1, Joseph Smith*, p. 461.

Made in the USA
Coppell, TX
21 September 2021